Inuit in Cyberspace

Neil Blair Christensen

Inuit in Cyberspace

Embedding Offline
Identities Online

Museum Tusculanum Press
University of Copenhagen
2003

Inuit in Cyberspace
Embedding Offline Identities Online

© Neil Blair Christensen & Museum Tusculanum Press 2003

Copy editor: Simon Frost
Consultants: Mark Nuttall and Frank Sejersen
Cover design and composition: Veronique van der Neut and the author
Set in ITC Legacy Serif
Printed in Denmark by Narayana Press, Gylling
ISBN 87 7289 723 6

Cover Photo from Kuujjuaq in Nunavik, Canada
Photographer: Scott Forrest

This publication has been made possible with the support of:

Aase og Jørgen Münters Fond
Folketingets Grønlandsfond
Nordea Danmark Fonden

Museum Tusculanum Press
Njalsgade 92
DK-2300 Copenhagen S
www.mtp.dk

Acknowledgements

I want to thank PhD Frank Sejersen, University of Copenhagen, and Professor Mark Nuttall, University of Aberdeen, for all their time and critical input into my research and subsequent writing of this book. My parents, Harry and Doreen Christensen, for their comments and feedback at all times. All the people who participated in the project and who took their time to think about and answer my questions; who let me nose around on their Web pages and fill up their inboxes with e-mail. I would also like to thank Marianne Alenius from Museum Tusculanum Press who took interest in this project and somehow found the patience to see it accomplished. I am grateful to all of you, without whom I could never have written this book.

"We can all too easily think of cyberspace and virtual reality in terms of an alternative space and reality"

Kevin Robins (1995:153)

"... despite mobility of residence – you always come from a place."

Susanne Dybbroe (1991:15)

Contents

Preface 9

Introduction: Shifting Boundaries 11
Modern tradition
Escape cyberspace
Old frontiers in new space

I Going Nowhere to get Everywhere 25
Online survey
E-mail interviews
Content analysis of Web pages
Wanted: practical method

II (Re)producing the Arctic in Cyberspace 45
The myth of cyberspace
Peripherality on the Net
Three regions: Canadian Arctic, Greenland and Alaska
Bridging a gap?

III A Common Web of Difference and Similarity 67
Recursive dynamics: social boundaries and cultural stuff
Us and them: self-identify by identifying others
Taloyoak in cyberspace
Native language
Guestbooks
Intelligible boundaries

IV Perceiving Cyberspace 97
Engaging with the world
Disengaging from abstract theory

Continuity? Accept Change and Understand Context 107

Appendix:

Survey results **114**

Notes **117**

References **123**

Preface

What you are about to read in this book is no more – it has changed. The events in the book certainly happened as described but the places you will be taken to, for the greater part, have altered. Some have become digital ruins, online ghost towns and curiosities, while others have disappeared. On the periphery of digital networks, dead links and missing Web pages are no more a loss to scientific standards of referencing and archiving, than an integer in our history of change. They disappear, as do billions of scribbles, conversations, and e-mails made every day on this planet. Some sites have become busy spaces with new infrastructures, new faces and new social networks. And even though alterations may have happened only a minute ago, these links and sites are nevertheless changed – most likely forever. What remains seems to be time and space, the frontiers that will always be final and the paradigm that gives us a sense of belonging. Thus, if space is the room we live in, be it social, geographic, economic or political, then time must surely be the measure by which we live.

As much as we would like to describe our common experience as total, it is doomed to be fragmented. As much as our lives seem to make an epitome of social boundaries that tell us apart, they are rather representations of interpenetration than separation. This book is a testimony to such an ongoing reality, where change and difference are the fundamental loci of human history, where new space cannot be produced or discovered if it does not accentuate difference. Even in the space of the utopian global village that digital fundamentalists preach to us as being a non-differentiating Darwinist step up the ladder, differentiation, as well as change of what once was, forms the very essence of their usage. Change and difference are not what separate or tear us apart but the constituents of what glues us together – the very dynamic of all social process. Without change and difference we are incognitos and thus we continuously seek new ways of representing and identifying ourselves, presenting ourselves to others in ways we deem appropriate. So if visualisation is the mirror of identification that we look into, checking for traffic as we move around in social space, it is also the window that allows others to see in. What is more, visualisation is now a 24-hour process, working when we sleep, eat or walk the streets. Our identities develop in *Lefebvrian* oceans, where colliding waves, energy and currents are constantly interpenetrating, changing and separating, even when we think we can isolate and divide them into distinct territorial waters. And when we do not notice, we have changed, or our surroundings have changed and thereby have changed us.

For French philosopher Henri Lefebvre, the spaces of visualisation are representational spaces that obey neither consistency nor coherence. They do, however, have practical impact on our lives because they are architectonic constructions, agents of social and political practice that link our understanding of objects and people through a knowledge that is always in the process of change. To cite what I will forever wish I had written, "No space disappears in the course of growth and development: the worldwide does not abolish the local" (Lefebvre 1991:86). I merely add, life continues. The Internet has not changed anything, but we have changed the ways in which we do many things by using the Internet. This book is a journey into how that happened at the advent of the Internet in the Arctic during the late 1990s and, as such, it is not meant as a prediction but as a help to our understanding. Enjoy the book.

Neil Blair Christensen, August 2002.

To my mother, Doreen Ceceile Christensen (1939–2002)

Introduction:
Shifting Boundaries

A hockey coach in Iqaluit, Canada, put up a Web site for the local club and received an e-mail from the recreational director of the Nuuk Municipality, the municipality for the capital of neighbouring Greenland, who was interested in advice on how to start a hockey league, something he found troublesome with only 15 players ranging in age from their mid-teens to 28. Consequently, it turned out to be cheaper for the Iqaluit players to fly to Nuuk for games than to Rankin Inlet, home of the closest Canadian adversary with a league of their own[1]. Several e-mails down the road, the two men started co-operating to establish an outdoor arena in Nuuk where the Iqaluit League may eventually play against Nuuk (Sackett 1998). When visiting the Iqaluit hockey Web page, one finds that the Iqaluit League is the only one to play 99.9% of their games at home. So, although the Internet is often related to buzzwords of the 1990s such as global village, information highway, virtual reality or e-commerce, many reasons for its success can be accounted for in less abstract and sometimes quite subtle everyday experiences.

FIGURE 1 A screen shot of the Iqaluit Amateur Hockey Association's Web page. Notice the syllabic text at the bottom of the logo [Web page] URL http://www.nunanet.com/~marcel/ [visit: June 14, 2000].

Modern tradition

It is my intention with this book to discuss the cultural and identity affirming use of the Internet amongst Inuit – mainly in relation to the Web[2]. During and after several months of fieldwork, I have found that some Inuit embed rather than disembed or deconstruct their identities and cultures on the Web. Thus, where media-hype, research and users seem to create, sometimes sensationalise, an absolute difference between what goes on when you are online compared to when you are offline, I have found an interest in de-mythicising the Internet a little, or at least in showing that there is a continuum, a resemblance or a connection between online cyberspace and offline space. Much of the social research on cyberspace investigates the disembodied potentials of this non-physical space to let people change between a multitude of identities or engage in online communities[3]. Instead, I investigate how cultural identities of Inuit are asserted on the Web by reference to their offline communities – a reference in which physicality plays a strong role.

In regard to the relation of technology and the dynamics of social organisation and culture, there exists a 'technology/culture' dichotomy that seems to earn sympathy amongst many (see Barglow 1994, Bauman 1998, Lanier 1990, Postman 1993). It connotes the idea of the fragmented and dissolute 'self' in the age of postmodernity, i.e. a world where people have lost social meaning and cultural significance, and are now gathering on the Internet to reproduce the social meaning of life: a process that increasingly empties offline space of social meaning and culture. According to a vision of Bauman, the powerful individuals on the Internet no longer need the empty shell we know as physical space because all their/its social meaning has been "transplanted into cyberspace" (1998:20). In cyberspace, however, transcendence rules, according to some, and people are devoid of physicality and matter because mind is separated from matter (Lanier 1990, Rheingold 1993, Springer 1991). Unfortunately, or luckily, this dreamworld, even if it sounds fascinating, cannot be used to analyse most Inuit Web pages as they are constructed with, quite contrary, strong links to offline sociality, culture and physicality such as landscape. The utopia of cyberspace is less represented in research now than it was 10 years ago, but it is, nevertheless, still the myth of cyberspace.

Thus, while most research on cyberspace is focusing on the construction and power of new (cultural) identities on the Internet, my approach is quite the opposite, focusing on examples where modern information technology is used to assert those cultural identities that already exist offline: what I choose to call offline culture[4]. Inuit identities and cultures are not statically bound to cultural characteristics that place them in a certain time and space of hunter-gatherers, but are continuously changing dynamically in relation to time, space and significance of meaning[5]. If culture is made significant and characterised through social relations, then it holds that culture is also signified where these social relations happen. The use of cyberspace as a space where cultural identity is asserted is an aspect of this dynamic adjustment and change in the (re)production of Inuit cultural identities.

I am not interested in glorifying Inuit or Arctic anthropologists as pathological culturalists, as much as I want to investigate the use of cyberspace that does not take on the role of a solitary cyber vacuum, distant from the world it actually exists within, but which instead is used to assert the world Inuit live in.

In much of the postmodern literature on cyber theory, I have come across analysis of cyberspace that I, in agreement with the ideas of Robins (1995), find abstract, romantic, mythic, transcendental, technophile or technophobic (see Benedikt 1991, Lanier 1990, Postman 1993, Rheingold 1993). However, in interviews with Inuit users and through analysis of Web pages that display a diverse range of Inuit cultural identities from across the Arctic, I have found descriptions and uses of cyberspace that are mostly of a specific, common and practical kind. Moreover, while some of the same cyber-scholars have a tendency to think of users within the singularity of non-space cyberspace, they produce images of the stereotyped *user* – a person who is disembodied and free of physical and cultural characteristics – who has momentarily freed his or her mind from matter. They seem to forget, nevertheless, that cultural identity is as mobile as the minds of the people who signify it with meaning. Thus, one should not automatically expect Inuit to use or relate to the Internet in the same manner as those European or American users who are the usual research subjects, nor should it be expected that all Inuit use or relate to the Internet in similar ways. Such perspectives disregard the ability of Inuit to use the Internet as another ordinary part of life in ways defined by themselves and adopted to local reality. The diversity of Arctic peoples is also reflected in the different experiences and attitudes that I encountered during my fieldwork to the relationships between culture, identity and technology. There is no such thing as a universal understanding of these relationships amongst Arctic peoples, and in many ways Web pages unfold their diversity.

In regard to the introduction of technology, Chance notes that while it has had an effect that is not purely positive, but rather two-sided, on Iñupiat – the Inuit of North Alaska – they "strongly disagreed with the notion that such an acceptance would result in the loss of their cultural way of life" (Chance 1990:xiv). Yet, Kawagley, a Yupiaq himself, regards modern/western technology to be disruptive for traditional knowledge and cultural ways of living (1995). Qitsualik, on behalf of Canadian Inuit, states that they have never regarded the technologies or tools of different cultures "with an 'ours' and 'theirs' mentality", but have remained utilitarian (Web document, year unknown). Thus, as discussed by Fienup-Riordan, there is much diversity amongst Inuit or Eskimos[6] reaching far beyond the usual igloo-dwelling stereotype (1990). Noticable in regard to this diversity are also the different ways that information technology is used in the different Arctic regions and communities – I will return to this issue several times throughout the book.

While my focus is on the assertion of offline culture and boundaries, I shall not fool myself, or the reader, into thinking that a contradictory study cannot be made. In this regard, the dynamics surrounding the use of technology are recursive, as noted by Postman: "Every technology is both a burden and a blessing; not either-or, but this-and-that" (1993:4-5). Thus, the point of argument here is that the use of Internet technology may very well lead to change of various aspects of culture such as language, social sphere or spirituality but which, at the same time, may just as well help to affirm and sustain the same or other aspects of the very same culture. Robins notes quite precisely that virtual interaction is about adjustment to the contemporary world (1995:147), rather than what often seems to be a theoretical deconstruction of the world in the age of postmodern theory. While this process of adjusting life is continuous, many seem to be discussing the Internet as a discontinuous phenomenon: either cherishing it as a revolution (utopians) or regarding it as a destroyer of that culture and social interaction which is not computer-mediated (dystopians). Common to many of these approaches is their tendency to describe cyberspace as an organism almost living its own life – a "Giant Worm" according to Lanier (1990) – feeding on its ability to attract people into a social vacuum cut off from offline life, severing the world into an active computer-mediated one and an empty physical one.

For that reason, part of my main focus is that human agency and networking seem to have disappeared in these sorts of discussions that operate within a paradigm of technological determinism: wondering what the Internet does or will eventually do, rather than what people already do and think. As held by Giddens, an institution – in my case the Internet – results from human agency, but is at the same time involved recursively as the medium of its production (1979:95). It is within such a self-determined, forced, individually as well as collectively generated world that a diverse range of Inuit cultural identities and social boundaries are asserted.

Although a reasonably new technology, the use of the Internet does not necessarily presuppose that its users take on new identities when presenting themselves through the medium, nor does it presuppose that offline cultures are mysteriously filtered away when people look into computer monitors or represent themselves in chat-rooms, guestbooks and Web pages. In a study by Dorais on modernity and identity in the Inuit community of Quaqtaq, a village in Nunavik[7] with some 250 residents, he notes that: "When combining 'traditionalism' and 'modernity,' Quaqtaq residents do not give the impression that they think they 'live in two different worlds,' as some aboriginal people have said they do (see for instance Kawagley 1995:vii)" (1997:104).

Consequently, if one speaks of Inuit tradition(s), one should not forget to speak of Inuit (post)modernity. Inuit have tradition within their (post)modernity, just as Europeans cherish their history without being any less European or modern. Fienup-Riordan concludes in her discussion on how Yup'ik Eskimos differ from the popular western image of peaceful igloo-dwellers that has been stereotyped to account for all Eskimos and Inuit that: "Contrary to the view that would see them as either traditional or modern, many Yupiit are ... striving to be both" (1990:231). With the risk of running up another generalisation, I believe that this goes for other Inuit as well. Whether or not this combination of modern and traditional is regarded to be successful varies in the opinions of the Inuit that I have corresponded with: nevertheless, the combination exists. In other words, contemporary Inuit are no less Inuit because of the technologies they use, the clothes they dress in, the hunting equipment they use or because they present themselves on a global arena such as the Web.

Cultural identities are not upheld in isolation but modulate in congruence with the rest of the world, whether in parts or as a whole – making sure that the cosmology or reality of any given society exceeds its own boundaries (Liep & Olwig 1993:39). Thus, identity is a relational process that potentially finds it ways across boundaries of space and through all aspects of life – even through the application and adaptation of a technology that is seen by many as the obliteration of offline culture. Yet the culture and identity asserting use of the Internet does not suggest that Inuit users are overly culturally guided as much as they engage in networks of relationships within, as well as outside of, their social group(s) – offline culture and identity does not always play an explicit role in these relationships. The dynamics between social relations and cultural assertion are recursive, even though they are not always equally represented.

Rachel Qitsualik, a Web site master, as well as the author of the column *Nunani* in Nunatsiaq News, suggests that the nomadic travelling spirit of Inuit, now being more or less trapped in small communities, could be part of the explanation for why Inuit and the Internet go so well together. The spirit could still be alive despite decades of more or less forced sedentarisation. Whereas Southerners with their agrarian traditions are at doubt how this nomadic technology will effect their social integrity, the Arctic case could be profoundly different, as Inuit feel a need to travel (Qitsualik, 1998:10). Even though it is a simplistic suggestion, try to imagine that now, promoted by the feeling of physical proximity on the Internet, Inuit can keep on travelling in a world that paradoxically seems to be expanding by becoming smaller.

The increase of imagined localisation beyond political and physical boundaries was expressed by two Inuit men from Iqaluit, Nunavut, during my research:

> "If we all have this similar kind of attitude of seeking facts and information in peaceful manner and intention(s), the more the whole world feels like home, no matter where we travel to and from." Male, Iqaluit, Nunavut, Canada (personal communication, 1998[8]).

> "In this time of high costs the Internet makes access to the world possible without having to leave home." Male, Iqaluit, Nunavut, Canada (personal communication, 1998).

The sense of home and belonging does not necessarily suffer from the increase of contact to the surrounding world. Instead, the process of juxtaposing 'us and them', when visiting foreign Web pages, helps to assert the sense of belonging. Indeed, even though the sense of home is generally described as something that is local, it is also asserted in places and situations that are located and take place far away. This goes for Inuit who visit Web pages made by people from far away, as well as those from far away who visit Inuit Web pages. Arctic images and reflections of physical and social space abound in great numbers on Arctic Web pages, thereby reproducing existing elements of language, culture, social and physical boundaries that are essential for (re)producing Inuit identity and culture. Thus, Inuit identity and culture are imaged and actively produced in cyberspace without being paradoxes between technology and culture forcing their way in opposite directions. By contributing with the creation of Arctic spaces for travels on the Web, Inuit are engaged in asserting rather than deserting their identity. In this regard, the Web is used and envisioned as a promoter of culture and identity rather than a postmodern filter pushing for the construction of new cyber-identities or cybercultures. This point has been put forward by Agre who states that "[a]s long as we focus on the limited areas of the Internet where people engage in fantasy play that is intentionally disconnected from their real-world identities, we miss how social and professional identities are continuous across several media, and how people use the several media to develop their identities in ways that carry over to other settings" (1999: paragraph 8). Instead of disembedding computer interaction from offline life, Inuit are generally embedding offline life into cyberspace, creating and asserting continuity in their lives – building on a continuum that has a strong influence in their world view conceptions without necessarily polarising reality into extremes of what is real or not. In regard to the world view of their Inuit ancestors, Burch states that: "extremes of time, space and existence were all seen as different points on a continuum, or as different phases or aspects of a single, unified whole, which was reality" (1988: 89).

A continuous reality that binds elements such as new information technology, tradition, language, identity, history and many more important aspects into a Web of self-determination that makes up some of the core elements of identity: not necessarily to sustain things as they are, but to carry on continuously and dynamically as any other vibrant culture does. Dahl argues that the dichotomy of culture and development arises when culture is separated from development, shifting the focus of development to a question of less culture – opposite to how we argue development (industrialisation) and culture in the West as a part of our cultural heritage (1986:15). The idea of lacking culture is explained by Fienup-Riordan as one where twentieth century westerners saw "Eskimos as strong, noble, independent and pure until corrupted by civilisation" (1990:16).

In regard to present day, Sejersen discusses the dilemma of authenticity where Inuit have to deal with environmental organisations who argue that development is counteractive to culture and indigenous rights (1998:240). In this image, culture becomes an adversary to the elements of industry and technology. In the 1970s and 1980s, environmentalist organisations like Greenpeace promulgated the idea that certain aspects of Inuit hunting, and thus culture and identity, were at times too modern or too traditional, and helped to make it apparent that Inuit were as much entangled in global processes as anybody else. Hunting with speedboats, rifles, ski-doos were concepts too modern for general western taste, while harpoons, kayaks and dog-sleds better fitted the western stereotype of Arctic peoples[9]. The process greatly undermined development and self-determination in the Arctic. Within such a context, Inuit experienced their existence to be tangled up in global or local strategies that originated far beyond their communities and it became increasingly important to have a choice of representing oneself in self-determined ways. Hence, many of the Arctic Web pages tell their own stories that confirm the urge of Inuit to inform and update others about the life in the Arctic regions – telling about home. The Web is not only used as a way of selling arts and crafts, attracting tourists, displaying organisations, institutions and individuals but also as a way of educating others, creating as little disinformation as possible:

> "... in the absence of words from the people living here, they [southerners] will feed on whatever happens to be available to them." Male, Nunavut, Canada (personal communication, 1998).

This is widely expressed in the keenness of Inuit to tell about themselves and their culture by answering both trivial and troublesome questions in discussion fora[10] as well as by imaging themselves audio-visually through text, pictures, maps and sound-clips on the Web. Generally speaking, Inuit wish to define or self-determine themselves rather than being defined by others, which blends well with the medium's ability to allow such contemporary self-promotion[11]. Generally speaking, Hannerz notes in regard to continuity of cultural change in local space and global process that: "this year's change is next year's continuity" (1996:28).

Following Inuit use of the Internet, their acceptance of the medium grows – a medium that is possibly the easiest and most effective so far in showing other people that Inuit are not vacuumed in a historical, cultural and traditional bubble, but that they are just as much contemporary and part of the world as anybody else without being any less Inuit or traditional because of their use of the Internet. In this regard, the idea of disembodiment, fragmented identities and space seems largely to be created by others.

Escape cyberspace

To summarise; I have several intentions, as the reader might have noticed by now, but they all attempt the clarification of processes wherein Inuit continuously (re)produce aspects of their culture and local space on the Web, whether these are social, physical, mental or otherwise. My research on local organisation, cultural identity and new technology connotes aspects of an already articulated policy by the Inuit Circumpolar Conference (1992:102):

> "New technologies introduced to the Arctic should first be assessed in terms of user acceptability, social and cultural impacts, and methods of implementing such technologies so as to contribute to and strengthen the culture of Inuit."

I hope to contribute with a discussion of how some Inuit use and relate to the Internet in specific, practical and everyday ways, as well as showing that researchers, media and public opinion often treat the Internet as an abstract organism, plastering it with causal visions and empty words that have promotional value but no actual substance to second them. It is my impression that many Inuit users generally seem to relate practically, circumstantially and contextually to their use of the network – reminding us that the Internet is socially propelled by people who live in physical space and use the Web because of various reasons such as practicality, entertainment or visions, rather than the more ideological or hallucinatory reasons that decision-makers and researchers argue over.

My approach takes on an old theme of cultural identity with a new perspective of cyberspace that currently lacks in Arctic anthropology, even though the Internet is of growing importance in Arctic societies and, as such, is taken seriously by many Inuit in the shaping, development and potentials of the region and the lives of the Inuit: selling a variety of local products through the Web, communication between citizen and government, long-distance education, telemedicine and enabling better and easier communication and services amongst people within and outside the region. The study is greatly motivated by the lack of social studies within the subject in regard to the Arctic[12]. Furthermore it is driven by a wish to relate a discussion about cyberspace to something more than cyberspace itself and to show that the groups who use the Internet are not always dependent on the medium for their existence as social groups, but can have an offline foundation as well. Thus, there is a focus on the elements of culture and identity that dilapidate a sometimes imagined gap between online and offline space.

Last, but not least, I find it important to show that the use of new technology by Inuit is not a peculiarity, nor a sensation, nor a corruption of culture, but a rather common part of a continuous (re)shaping and integration of old and new elements in the lives of the Inuit. The amount of technology in the daily lives of Inuit make them no less fully fledged Inuit than before, unless they themselves feel so. Nevertheless, it might help them to reach more people directly in the relational (re)shaping of Inuit identity. This is important to stress in a world where one is often confronted by people who statically regard Inuit as such only when they ride their dog-sleds, hunt wildlife, use their kayaks and build igloos, but see them as culturally amputated and threatened when viewed in company with computers, motor vehicles or western clothing. From another perspective, Friedman's example of *La Sape* is apt, where young men in the Congo dress in western designer clothes without feeling social disattachment or loss of culture (1995:87). Somehow similar; Inuit using the Internet do not necessarily experience a loss of culture or traditional knowledge, unless one considers these to be what Friedman refers to as "static museological objects". Identity, culture, tradition and (post)modernity are continuously (re)defined and affirmed; Pullar concludes in his account on the revitalisation of Alutiiq culture and ethnic identity (1992:189): "Our culture may change but it will never die."

Old frontiers in new space

As made clear by Michel de Montaigne:

> "A man may well have detailed knowledge or experience of the nature of one particular river or stream, yet about all the others he knows only what everyone else does; but in order to trot out his little scrap of knowledge he will write

a book on the whole of physics! From this vice many great inconveniences arise" (Montaigne [1533-1592] 1995).

This study is an anthropological attempt to describe and discuss the practical and culture-specific rather than abstract attitude of many Inuit towards the Internet, which I experienced during the online fieldwork undertaken throughout most of 1998. Naturally, not every participant relates the use of the Internet in similar or overly cultural ways. Many Inuit also conceive the Internet as culturally destructive, a trend, as an entertainment tool, a place to engage in Internet Relay Chat (IRC) or in MUD/ MOO[13], as a natural part of their work or school or in some cases a medium to surf for nude pictures:

"People talk about the negative effects of TV, but to me the Internet is TV squared in terms of Inuit culture getting overwhelmed by outside influences." Male, Nunavut, Canada (personal communication, 1998).

I focus on the aspects of Inuit use that affirms offline cultural identity; not because the specific theme is necessarily more significant than other aspects of cyberstudies – which it is not – but because most research already dealing with culture and cyberspace deals with culture and social groups that are based on the same medium for their existence. It is my opinion that such "cyberism" willing or unwillingly helps to sustain conceptions of cyberspace as a vacuum or a solitary reality rather than as a space of life that is organised in relation to the world people live in. While the economic, democratic, political and identity-constructive potentials of cyberspace are highlighted and revolutionised by media and decision makers over and over again as being real, the aspects of identity on the Internet are mostly associated with worlds of fantasy and the ability to do whatever you want to. The secretive aspects of creating a new identity or hiding a real identity in cybersex, MUDs and IRC are much more investigated[14].

The use of the Internet is constantly changing and the ability and wish of some people to use the Web actively without having to take on highly situational identities or engaging in online subcultures does exist: not least because of a diversification of users during the last 10 years, technological developments in the Web, infrastructure, computer hardware and software. But then again, this does not mean that the same people cannot engage in these virtual activities and still use some of their time on affirming offline cultural values. The Internet is not necessarily a space to hide in, nor is it a space that mysteriously filters away the cultural identities of peoples.

In the research done for this study, I have found that many Inuit are using the Web to present accurate images of how they conceive themselves. Yet, the different ways they do so and the different stereotypes that are sometimes invoked on Web pages are not what fully constitutes them and, most importantly, no two pages are alike. There is much more to life in the Arctic than what is revealed on those Web pages that process the art of representation and identity assertion. Some Inuit Web pages are thus constructed with the use of stereotype images such as igloos, snow, dogs, fur clothed Inuit and icebergs, which are recognised by outside viewers, but have textual content that display the cultural diversity of many groups: Iñupiat, Yup'ik, Inuvialuit, Kalaaallit, Inuit and Sikumiut, mostly combined with a reference to local space. The relations between outside and inside members are evident in the construction of the Web pages that use stereotypes to attract global attention and those that have more specific content about local life in the Arctic.

Writing dramatically, and quite falsely, that the Inuit inhabit "a land as empty and inhospitable as Mars … about to cross the ice bridge to the 21st century" (Teitelbaum 1997) does not lie within the motivation of this study – although it sounds exciting. Instead, it is my hope that this study contributes with some non-sensationalist and rather common descriptions of how some Inuit are shaping or defining the Internet in ways intrinsic to what it means to be Inuit as well as live in the Arctic, while being computer-mediated actors on a growing worldwide social scene.

Albeit the examples provided in this study might be accused of giving a somehow one-sided picture of Inuit Web use as cultural, one should notice that the general picture is quite varied and contested. There is much difference in the extent to which Inuit in the regions of

Arctic Canada, Alaska and Greenland use the Web. The use of Web pages to assert cultural and local identity is much less evident on pages from Alaska and Greenland compared to the Canadian material. However, Greenlandic pages often present national, local or political identities rather than ethnic identities as is often the case with Web pages related to Nunavut. In Canada, the coming about of Nunavut seems to be a major reason for people's wish to represent themselves culturally. Almost any Web page from Nunavut with respect for 'itself' is constructed to link to several other Nunavut Web pages representing boards, government and organisations. Another difference is the local diversity of content in Web pages. Accordingly, when Web pages are constructed as semi-mirrors of local communities, organisations, businesses, municipalities or individual 'selves', the diversity shows. The concept of 'otherness' is not only a marker in the social relations between Inuit and others but it also acts as a way of asserting local identity and regional difference amongst Inuit[15]. Thuesen, for example, finds that associations in the Greenlandic towns of Sisimiut and Maniitsoq sometimes exaggerate the marking of difference through symbols to the point where the object of the association seems less important (1991:52).

The existence of Web pages that assert offline cultural identity partially question in practicality some of the theoretical concerns that people such as Postman (1993) have in regard to the ability of people to withstand the obliteration of their cultural identities by technology. Yet, in terms of identity and culture there seems to be a recursive construction and deconstruction of identity going on: social processes that define the changes within a new context of meaning depending on the situation – just as some Inuit do by entering the Web with cultural identities. I draw on different examples from the Web to describe and discuss the assertion of local and cultural identity (meanings of belonging), but it is impossible to encompass the full amount of growing material. I cannot guarantee that the Web pages I refer to have not changed or even disappeared, but this mirrors with amazing clarity the dynamics of identity assertion.

I

Going Nowhere to Get Everywhere

Imagine if an anthropologist travelled to the Arctic with a luggage full of shorts, malaria pills and a tropical helmet, or went to the tropics with sealskin muffs, long woollens and warm boots. It figures by lucid reasoning that the equipment one uses somehow configures to the space in which one travels. In the case of this study, some of the major equipment and supplies needed for my cyberspace travel were a connected computer, plenty of electricity, money for the phone bill and a comfortable chair.

My own position is one of mixed Danish-Jamaican parentage, but I was born in Illoqqoortoormiut, East Greenland, and I lived in Uunarteq (Cape Tobin), East Greenland, in Pituffik (Dundas), North Greenland, and in Nanortalik, South Greenland, until the age of eight when the family moved to Denmark. I grew up with the practicalities of social boundaries that were Greenlandic, Jamaican and Danish, and I believe I have gathered personal experience in the dynamics of cultural identity and social boundaries from early on. In regard to the Internet, I got my first computer and e-mail account in 1995 and I started using the Web in 1997.

The example of a comfortable chair in Denmark, and later Scotland, for fieldwork about Arctic peoples is one that is likely to foster grey hairs on the head of many an experienced anthropologist. Paccagnella summarises the hardship with wit and humour in the title *Getting the Seats of Your Pants Dirty* (1997) for his paper on virtual communities and cyber anthropology. Pickard notes in the title of a chapter on ethnography in cyberspace that the researcher is *Always Home For Tea* (1998). One method among the many available to the researcher could be defined as "... the ethnographic study of boundaries between humans and machines that are specific to late 20th century societies" (Escobar 1994:216).

Without doubt somebody will object to this cyber anthropological method and label it as insubstantial, or argue how very limited a perspective such fieldwork is determined to provide. Nevertheless, I decided it would be a good approach for a study on the use of cyberspace in the Arctic.

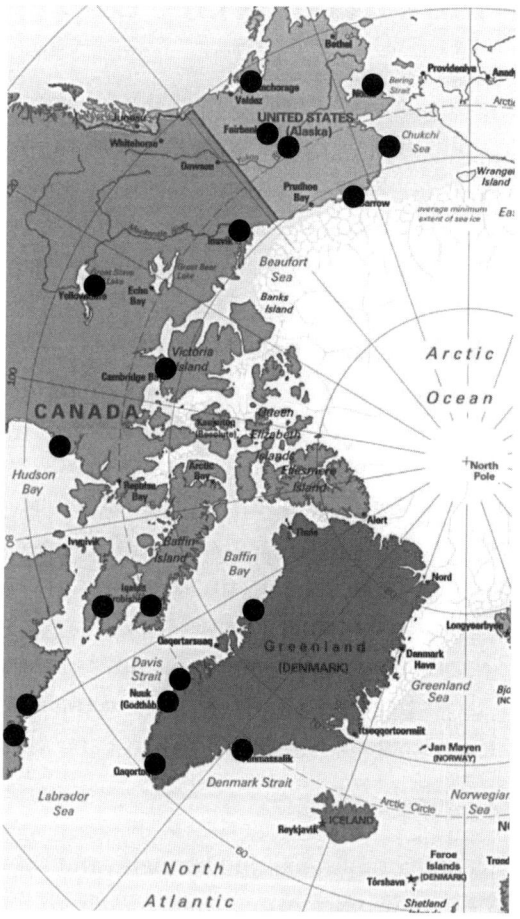

FIGURE 2 Locations of Inuit web users who participated in my online pilot survey - some of which also participated in e-mail interviews. The locations on the map only cover those users who provided information on their whereabouts. The communities on the map are:

Alaska: Anchorage, Barrow, Delta Junction, Fairbanks, False Pass, Uminak Island (outside map), Nome.
Canada: Cambridge Bay, Happy Valley, Inuvik, Iqaluit, Nain, Pangnirtung, Rankin Inlet, Yellowknife.
Greenland: Maniitsoq, Nuuk, Qaqortoq, Upernavik, Tasiilaq.

Other Inuit web users participated from locations outside the map such as Copenhagen and Ottawa. I did my research from Copenhagen, Denmark as well as Aberdeen, Scotland.

As case-studies have elucidated, fieldwork in physical space has no foolproof method for understanding people in the right way, nor is it my intention here to deliver proof of such a case. As known from Malinowski's diary and work (1922, 1967), fieldwork is not without difficulties, no matter how much one tries to prepare for it[16].

Since the days of Malinowski, with the change of time, conception and ideology, the expected space of fieldwork has extended towards the home of the anthropologist and thus away from the more exotic environments. As put by Sejersen, we now have the opportunity to do remote fieldwork at home: a process that revolves around the exotification of anthropologists' own cultures[17]. The space of work has followed the changes in conception of space in general. As the world has been explored and found, some anthropologists have come to realise that the sealed and confined space they went searching for does not really exist – that the world as a whole is as big at home as it is abroad. Hence, Olwig & Hastrup discuss how space and place have moved from being *fixed co-ordinates* in the ethnographic map to realising that people, including anthropologists *move*. With the anthropological loss of place as a metaphor for culture, anthropology is now allowed to capture mobility, which involves *deterritorialisation* and *reterritorialisation* (Escobar 1994:228, Olwig & Hastrup 1997). A phenomenon that depends on the TimeSpace compression of advanced communication technology to potentialise cultures without territories (Featherstone 1995:115). This has not only been advanced, from a theoretical point of view, through a change in anthropological self-interest and research, but is also related to the increasing ease of communication between many parts of the world. According to Clark, this enlarged spatial horizon has from a historical point of view been an ongoing process from the early days of anything fuelling geographical discovery (1992:60), thus preceding the development of anthropological theory and practise by far. The combined assertion of place and culture on Web pages are part of the reterritorialisation, however, that maintain the importance of place for Inuit culture. The Arctic is so different from other places in the world, that it is imperative for the assertion of Inuit identities - also on Web pages.

Yet, the increasing ease in communication and widespread social contact can be a very relative one in comparison to the theoretical and practical questions that arise from extensive use of non-physical environments for interviews and research. The constantly discussed merits of understanding people the right way – if it can be put like that – are likewise relevant in cyberspace. The research and fieldwork preceding this study were, for a greater part, dependent on excessive access to a computer, e-mail interviews, Internet survey and online literature or references. This, among things, was needed to enable correspondence with people thousands of miles away, spread out in an area stretching from the Aleutians in the Bering Strait, across Arctic Alaska and Canada, to Eastern Greenland (see map). Even though grasping a very big area, the methods chosen were in no way an easy way out, as much as they were an easy way in.

A predicament in this type of research of which I have come across are the limitations and hardships the medium gives in establishing confidence among the participants towards the scope of the research and my person. The physical distance does not unshackle the anthropologist from having to secure a certain trust among the participants: just as it should be, one may add.

Conducting interviews per e-mail sometimes turned out to be a mental minefield for both respondent and researcher, as it was often necessary to imagine the situation a respondent was referring to, where the person was coming from, not only physically but also mentally and ideologically. It is a method and a forum where the semantics are indeed explicit in form of written statements, but very implicit without the nod of a head, a sigh of relief or a shrugging shoulder to emphasise meaning – where the computer screen helps to create a de-polarisation of space and dithers body language (Baudrillard 1993:19). It is a space where there is paid greater attention to the written word than the spoken word. Condensing thought and argument might be a well-tried method in academic writing, but is not necessarily so in the fieldwork interview. Yet, it can both limit discussion and spontaneity compared to a face-to-face situation, as well as providing conciseness and time to think about answers in a text-written environment. In regard to face-to-face contact and cyberspace, Featherstone and Burrows find that social life operates with an "implicit physiognomic notion that the face and the body are the only 'true' sources that can reveal the character of a person" (1995:5). For this reason, among others, it is possible to find pictures of Web masters on their Web pages.

During my research, preliminary results were made available for participants at my research Web site, and they[18] were invited to read, comment on and criticise the results of research they featured in. However, only a handful of interviewees responded with comments after having read my findings. I do not know how many actually made use of this opportunity, but still, as noted by one, the speed of feedback between researcher and researched seemed to uphold some potential in comparison with that of previous methods:

> "I think a final version of a research paper can be on the desk of a client in less time than in the past if all the principle research are [sic] on line, like in our situation." Male, Canada (personal communication, 1998).

The method chosen clearly kept out computer non-users from becoming directly involved in the fieldwork: a noted and discussed dilemma in cyber anthropology (see Hamman 1998). Several participants were aware of the privilege of access, as well as the pitfalls of possible polarisation:

> "My fear is that it will only be used by the wealthy of our society." Male, Qaqortoq, Greenland (personal communication 1998).

> "If it is to be more useful more Inuit need to get online." Male, Nunavut, Canada (personal communication 1998).

> "My major concern is that many people in Alaska and elsewhere in the world do not have access to the same information." Female, Barrow, Alaska (personal commu-nication 1998).

Although I shall not deal much with the following aspect, a quick glimpse at the ISERIT Web directory of Greenlandic Web pages[19], reveals that the majority of Web pages are made by men rather than women. The majority of Web pages that I have browsed during research are also mastered by men. However, there seems to be no visible difference in the content of the pages or its presentation because of the producer's gender[20]. Whether one chooses to call this an effect of disembodiment or transcendency will have to remain an open-ended question as it has not fallen within the direct scope of this book.

Had there been sufficient funds available, non-users could have been included but, as this was not the case, it was chosen to rely upon users since they were accessible through the Internet. As I have argued on another occasion[21], the current users are among the ones to play a pivotal role in the acceptance, incorporation and development of the Internet in the Arctic, as they are representatives of the reasons and incentives influencing the past, present and future use of the Internet and other ICTs. The methods of research were not chosen only in response to previous anthropological, sociological, geographic or ethnographic cyberstudies but were also very much for economic and practical reasons. Economically, it was impossible to plan and conduct this type of research with face-to-face interaction covering such a vast region for a student without proper funding – the situation I found myself in at the time. The apparent thing to do was to use the subject of research for research and let the anthropologist or ethnographer become part of the field – in short, do what you study. With fieldwork in computer-mediated space somehow similar to my own, Turkle had previously described her own method of studying online communities as one where "... I lived within worlds new to me, tried to understand what they are about, and tried to write about my understandings so that the worlds I studied could come alive for others" (1984:315). In the same way as if one were to study how people hunt or engage in subsistence activities, it would be reasonable to go hunting with them or otherwise view these subsistence activities[22].

As a way of giving something from my experience back to the researched – besides research papers and pilot survey results that could seem too abstract to some – I maintained a comprehensive resource directory of Arctic Web pages[23] that was – and still is – hoped to be of use for those Web users who have an interest in the Arctic on the Web. The dialogue between Web users and myself greatly developed my own knowledge and thoughts on the use of the Internet. But not all users were interested in the focus on cultural identity that gradually developed and often seemed much more interested in the development of economy and infrastructure in regard to the Internet, or were just plain interested in their own personal use. My focus, notwithstanding, was already broad enough when considering all the cultural diversity of the Arctic peoples by whom I refer to some as Inuit. While I have chosen to keep cultural identity and social boundaries as my focus, the reader is reminded that this is merely a broad perspective amongst many others in regard to the Internet and one wherein there is much cultural diversity online as well as offline.

In the case of my fieldwork, I would be studying the use of cyberspace in cyberspace but, as it should be noted, this was naturally supplemented by literature and work in the physical space of Copenhagen, Denmark, and Aberdeen, Scotland, as well. Certainly, this fieldwork without face-to-face contact had limitations from the very beginning, as there were no physical gestures to guide my understanding of the statements made by the respondents.

Furthermore, the research environment was not only text-written but also English – or else Danish, as some Greenlanders preferred. Without question, this prevented not only non-users from participating but also people who were not confident or able to write and express themselves through those written languages. This presents a serious problem in regard to the methods used here, but I reminded myself that the anthropologist in the physical environment in a similar way often relies more on the orally advantaged or the powerful for information. At least this method gave people time to formulate themselves. This is no excuse for the apparent shortcoming but it points out, to some extent, that the dilemma is relevant to most anthropological fieldwork.

Online Survey

The use of Internet survey is, among others, described by Coomber (1997) in relation to his online survey of drug dealers that led him to 80 informants in 14 countries from four continents. He concludes that there are certain benefits in using the Internet when trying to research people who are difficult to reach or when research is of a sensitive nature.

I certainly benefited from the communicative compression of distance and users themselves exemplified some of the potentials:

> "I hope the world will become even smaller, especially when living in such a remote location as Greenland. The Internet really opens up the world." Male, Greenland (personal communication, 1998).

> "Internet will open the world for people living in remote areas." Male, Nuuk, Greenland (personal communication, 1998).

> "We are not Inuit, but Inupiat, and are rapidly learning to use our connectivity to establish relationships, both personal and professional outside our immediate geographical locations." Male, Point Hope, Alaska (personal communication, 1998).

Yet, the greatest predicament of conducting an Internet survey (see appendix) is the same as when offline: namely, how to ask the right questions and listen carefully. As I was new to the field and did the survey as much out of curiosity as actually knowing what I was specifically looking for, I would admit that many questions were addressed incorrectly. This was painfully referred to by a handful of respondents as well. However unfortunate this was, my flagrant questions were partially designed to be on purpose. I was the researcher who had just arrived in a new environment, just starting to get an idea about what was interesting. I did not want to premeditate the later line of discussion that I was counting on and so, by asking broadly, I hoped to come across something of the sort – it was intended as a kind of "processual approach to fieldwork"[24]. Most of all, the survey gave me a user profile of the people whom I was later to interview, which in the end made it more than a positivist record of opinions and facts. The voluntary and hence representational feature of an online survey can be a troublesome one but, in this case, the outcome of the survey was foremost a point of contact to Inuit Web users and their user profiles.

I first started out with four notions about the design of the survey. 1) Questions should not take long to answer, as they might make the respondent leave, from pure boredom, which had been pointed out in other studies as well (Pitkow & Recker 1994, Smith 1997). 2) The medium gave the respondent anonymity and thus little obligation to complete a questionnaire. The questions therefore should be understandable for young people and people who did not speak English as their native tongue. 3) The questions should allow for both quantitative questions to speed up the process and qualitative questions to provide some substance and let people express themselves. 4) The Web pages were to be constructed light, so people in remote areas with slow network connections could also view them without stopping data transmission in frustration. In addition to these four points, I decided to use the survey to ask people for their e-mail address and invite them to discuss further through subsequent e-mail correspondence. After my Web pages were in place, on March 10, 1998, I sat at the computer for 22 hours tracking every e-mail address on the Web with affiliation to the Arctic communities that I could find. This counted well above 1,000. My initial, exploratory e-mail contained the following message:

> "I'm a graduate student from the University of Copenhagen, Denmark, doing some research on the use of Internet in the Arctic. The Project is called "Inuit in Cyberspace" and I need you, the users of the Internet, to help me. So if you can spare 2–3 minutes, please visit my place at http://www.geocities.com/Athens/Oracle/9724/[25] and you'll make my day. Make my day! Neil Blair Christensen, Institute of Eskimology, University of Copenhagen Denmark."

Within half an hour, the first submission arrived from Nunavut, in Canada. Out of 131 respondents, 70 supplied their e-mail address. This was possibly the biggest success of the survey[26] as it supplied me with more and better information than a two minute survey could ever have done and thus enabled ten months of correspondence and fieldwork. After two months the survey had quietened down with only a couple of submissions each month: still, the questionnaire will remain on the Web as it still serves as a point of contact for users.

The results of my online survey conducted in 1998 showed that the actual use of the Internet on user-level was versatile and revolved around e-mail, surfing and representation through Web pages. Other or more specified reasons were research, work, school or activities related to entertainment: being everything from watching pornographic material, playing network-games as well as gathering information for hobbies like recipes for cooking. The average person had started using the Internet in 1994, some changing from Local Area Networks (LAN) or Municipal Area Networks (MAN) to Wide Area Networks (WAN) as the Internet developed, gradually going from UseNet and e-mail to the use of WWW as it developed further. Although 39 per cent had access through work, only 16 per cent of these people actually used it for work. Those using it for work did so in a number of ways, many overlapping each other. Examples were maintaining Web pages, information and public relation, providing Internet services and Web page design, e-mail for easy and fast communication, WWW for information gathering vital to work, financial transactions, online or long-distance teaching and different ways of system administration. According to the answers of respondents, no specific geographic region utilised any of these ICTs in any remarkably different way from others on regional levels. However, many ICTs were more abundant in larger communities, where work relating to specific skills was to be found, than in small communities. Thus most people using the Internet at work were situated in bigger communities.

In regard to possible gain from the Internet, 46 per cent replied that individuals gained most from the Internet, followed by communities (31), corporations (17) and organisations (6). It confirms that the Internet in the Arctic is not yet being used efficiently for business/e-commerce, although there is quite a high level of business representation on Web pages. This was also endorsed by the majority of people who used the Internet at work (leisure and work) but who did not list corporations as the ones to gain the most. This statement came mostly from people who did not use the Internet or ICTs for work, whether it was as in a manner of business, organisation or otherwise. A total of 43 per cent regarded the Internet as something that promoted business, opposed to 40 per cent stating it promoted culture. The last 17 per cent thought the Internet was overrated. Whatever truths the myth about business and prosperity entail as concerns the Internet, they were not seriously endorsed by the responses from people. In later interviews my questions on the particular issue of e-commerce were only answered by those who were on the customers side of things. There was an overall deficiency of information or experiences related to economic profit via the Internet. The substantial amount of Web sites offering online ordering, especially in Canada, however, indicate that this is a perspective that could be taken up in another study. In regard to gaining from the Internet in categories of individual, community, corporations and organisation, 66 per cent agreed that success of one of the above-mentioned categories would benefit the others. The utilisation, and one should suppose the benefits, of the Internet occurred foremost in the big communities and settlements:

> "The cost and infrastructure are such that those who would possibly benefit the most (i.e. in the extreme remote communities) do not have ready access to the technology." Female, Yellowknife, Canada (personal communication, 1998).

A total of 60 per cent agreed that the Internet brings development to the Arctic, while 20 per cent did not know and 20 per cent did not agree. The development these respondents had in mind was often related to future perspectives and not so much related to an already experienced development. The current development was explained within technological discourse, rather than a human perspective – meaning, "what technology has done for us" rather than "what have we done with technology." There was a tendency to approach the Internet in terms of what could be done with it in a future sense, linked with the development of even better technology. The development of the Internet needed for this was to be promoted through partnership of government and private enterprise, according to 75 per cent. A regional difference appeared here, making Alaska most receptive to development through private investments, Canada through partnership and Greenland through government only: differences that correspond well with both the different economic as well as political structures of the three regions and their ways of providing Internet services.

To summarise the basic survey outcome once more, the people responding did so mainly from larger communities, they were employed and had used ICTs for a number of years. Respondents were seldom novices to the medium of the Internet and so the novelty of Web had worn off for the majority. Many supported the argument that the Internet brings development to the Arctic, but not automatically a development of homogeneity, democratisation, or physical togetherness in the Arctic region. Although many were aware of the pan-Arctic potential in the Internet for Inuit, few had any current examples of personal use that resembled their ideas for the Arctic as a co-operating region. Generally, they were much more keen to write about local or regional issues. In fact a respondent replied

> "As it is now, the use of the Internet and information and communication between Arctic people is accidental." Male, Maniitsoq, Greenland (personal communication, 1998).

E-mail Interviews

In Hamman's *Cyberorgasms* about online sex in chat rooms, he describes how narrow bandwidth resulted in some misinterpretations (1996:11). Narrow bandwidth is meant as a metaphor for the limitation that text-based environments give the researcher. In one particular example, Hamman misunderstands a female he is about to interview as inviting him to online sex, also called cybersex.

In many ways I encountered similar problems in my research. They had nothing to do with sex, I should add, but were related to the earlier mentioned missing intonation of a statement, the twinkle in an eye, the shrugging of shoulders or any other physical gesture that was not apparent in a text-written environment unless it was pointed out through signs like :-) , :-(, ;-) , verbalised sounds, explicitly foul or wordy language. This made e-mail correspondence very repetitive from time to time.

If I addressed a question, I would sometimes have to explain the detailed circumstances for asking it. I would send off the questions and receive replies that made me wonder whether my question had been understood in the way it was intended. This would result in my reshaping the question and sending it back to the same person or several others. Indeed, I got the feeling that respondents believed I was only interested in answers that satisfied my ideas, while making life miserable for other people – not my intention, which was rather the search for valid results. However, the search annoyed or demanded too much time from some people to the point where communication ceased. To be honest, I do not blame them, as I would surely have done the same had it not been for the need to broaden the understanding of the semantics involved into something more substantial.

In another case, North notes in the use of e-mail interviews for his study on the Internet and the UseNet that the extra work required by a subject for writing an answer rather than engaging in an informal face-to-face interview is an imposition (1994:7). The possibility of quickly reformulating one's question does not always exist in the use of e-mail and so it can become a tedious business for both researcher and researched to conduct this type of interview. In many occurrences in my fieldwork, people would read their e-mail three or four times each week and thus it could easily take a week for a reply to arrive. Add to that the repetition of clarifying questions and I was looking at three to four weeks, in extreme cases, to get a question and its surrounding areas answered and clarified. Prompted by a newspaper debate in the two Greenlandic newspapers *Atuagagliutit* and *AvangÂmiok*[27] that took place over a period of nine years from 1911 to 1920 with some 30 letters about Greenlandic identity and nationality, I convinced myself that three to four weeks was a relatively short period of time for written correspondence. In the days of the particular newspaper debate, only people living in Nuuk and Qeqertarsuaq – hometowns for the newspapers – were able to get their letters printed in the newspaper and read them on a regular basis. People in the rest of Greenland had to wait for their annual supply of newspapers dating back a year.

Admittedly, in my case, my laziness from time to time prolonged the process as well, and also my questions, especially in the beginning, were very likely not always precise enough. Swift responses that at times gave the impression of limited physical distance were rare and, as time took its toll, it seemed, from my point of view at least, as if the bandwidth became even more narrow when I was longing for replies but did not want to risk bothering people excessively. The obstacles this process presented could possibly have been avoided through face-to-face contact. Nevertheless the written transcripts proved to be assets in situations where swift talk, physical gestures or scribbled notes could have been misinterpreted just as readily. Moreover, having the opportunity to re-address questions to informants via e-mail, when it turns out during write up that not all the essential questions have been asked in the field, would benefit every researcher. The fieldwork does not end with your departure from a given community and potentially continues, every time you check your e-mail.

The physical distance and the comfort of "home sweet home" with all its books, references and people to seek advice from does not necessarily, at least in my case, prevent one from making mistakes. As a result, the feeling of stress, anxiety or frustration from conducting fieldwork in a computer-mediated space is not much different – to my knowledge – from experiencing fieldwork in physical space. However, the merits of uncertainty or reassurance tend to be extrapolated by physical distance. Having a cup of coffee with an informant is an unlikely scenario in cyberspace, yet so is receiving a written answer the length of an essay from an informant for the anthropologist in the physical field. The lack of physicality does alter the mutual perception between researcher and researched, but instead of determining it as a lack, compared with physical fieldwork, I have chosen to accept these circumstances for this type of online fieldwork[28]. All depending on the scope of research, the degree of physicality is more important to some researchers than to others. In my case, I maintain that the lack of funding more than anything else prohibited my use of face-to-face interviews.

Content Analysis of Web Pages

The study of Web pages is often, at least initially, likely to happen in full anonymity. Not only do the researched Web masters (the ones who make the Web pages) not experience the somewhat intrusive character of an anthropologist, but they also have no idea that they are being studied – a method that Bernhard characterises as "unobtrusive observation" (1988:290). Under some circumstances these methods can pose ethical dilemmas having to do with the right of communities and individuals to have a say in what sort of research they are included in.

The contents of Web pages were in many cases studied without the Web masters or communities knowing about it. However, as the content on the pages represents public published material, I do not quite see this as an ethical threat or even intrusive to the point of an ethical dilemma – basically, the material is there to be seen and scrutinised. Nevertheless, I have discussed many of the following matters with some of the Web masters and some of the users of their pages[29]. Further, there has been given consent by the authors of Web pages that are shown in screenshots throughout this publication and it should be noted that some of the pages studied are maintained by respondents in the e-mail interviews, thus allowing me to discuss content, design and purpose with them. The Web pages that were not discussed, were so either because of limited time and resources on my behalf or because of reasons such as lack of time, interest or resources on behalf of the Web masters. Also, in regard to official sanction, it seems equally interesting to consider whether the Web masters have the consent of the communities and the people that they sometimes represent. But, as this particular aspect is not dealt further with here, and as it will later show, representation of Inuit on the Web is in the hands of few, of whom not all are Inuit. Yet many of these Web pages assert diverse Inuit social boundaries and cultural identities, often doing so in ways that currently do not differ much from the Web pages made by Inuit.

> "We view public discourse on CMC [computer-mediated communication] as just that: public. Analysis of such content, where individuals', institutions' and lists' identities are shielded, is not subject to 'Human Subject' restraints.

> Such study is more akin to the study of tombstone epitaphs, graffiti, or letters to the editor. Personal? – yes. Private? – no." (Rafaeli, as quoted in Sudweeks & Rafaeli, 1995).

The material on the Web is published to be seen, used and mentally digested. I am of the opinion that this particular conception should not be confused with use of transcripts from chatrooms, MUD and MOO, which is rightfully addressed as presenting an ethical dilemma at times[30].

Studies on the use and importance of Web pages have for a majority centred around the establishment of a genre for different Web pages[31]. These genres have generally been established on grounds that: "... individuals will typically express similar social motives, themes and topics in a communication with similar physical and linguistic characteristics (i.e. form), that is, they will communicate in a recognised genre" (Crowston & Williams 1997:3).

Thus, where genre theory is more focused on the typological framework of a series of pages, I am interested in the social framework. The former I regard to be static, the latter dynamic. The culturally related contents of some Inuit Web pages do not always coincide with their main purpose (their genre). Hence, the Iqaluit Hockey Association's Web site has syllabic characters in its logo but does not display much else that makes one think of cultural identity: i.e. the main purpose is to represent the hockey club rather than Inuit. Nevertheless, as a symbol of identification, the syllabics are still there.

A Greenlandic Web page such as the home page of KalaK, aka Ulrik Motzfeldt, displays a logo that is red and white, resembling the Greenlandic flag cut in half with the text "KalaK Greenland", and has a small tourist guide as well as a guestbook. It even welcomes visitors in seven different languages by the use of a rolling banner. It would probably fit a genre type called 'personal home page' but it is not my main concern to find out its type as much as it is to analyse its content and socially negotiated meaning. By avoiding genre methodology, I get to choose examples from a wider and thus more representative selection of Web pages. The selecting and assessment of Web pages have characterised the method of genre, to use the words of Chandler (1997a:paragraph 6), as a "theoretical minefield". The characteristics, so to speak, under my attention are the ones relating to social boundaries: the symbols and the statements that can be found on Inuit Web pages. Although I look in some cases into how they are linked to each other, I analyse the Web masters' reasons for design and links instead of trying to divide their products into different types – rather, the focus is action-based. This method shows that not only are the reasons for certain Web page content versatile beyond typology but also that these reasons are very different in the Arctic from place to place and from person to person, both on the Web and in physical space.

I hope that this line of approach contributes to the humanification of the study of Web pages in a time where research seems very much focused on the pages rather than the people who make them. Few of the current studies undertaken on Web pages seem to have drawn on the conceptions of the producers (Web masters) or viewers of these pages. However, as described by Walters in her thesis on purposes and forms of personal Web pages, "[m]uch of the coding, of necessity, was subjective; in particular, identifying the purpose of the homepage and the nature of the links were difficult" (1996:7). The identification of genres for home pages is usually carried out through listing/coding certain key features and to some extent this is also done here: e.g. whether or not the Web pages have anything to do with Inuit. Then again, I have found many Web pages to be a mix of several genres, so the method is not used intensely here, unless one considers identity affirming pages as a genre. Also, instead of pinpointing a definite purpose for a Web page and the nature of its links, I think it is more important, in regard to a study on identity, to acknowledge that identity and social boundaries are dynamic. As put by Cohen on the situational use of symbolic boundaries and stereotypes:

> "... the boundary as the community's public face is symbolically simple; but, as the object of internal discourse, it is symbolically complex ... In its 'public' face, internal variety disappears or coalesces into a simple symbolic statement. In its 'private' mode, differentiation and variety proliferate, and generate a complex symbolic statement" (1986: 13).

Thus, there are differences in the stereotypes that an out-group member, a researcher like myself, will use in the title "Inuit in Cyberspace" and the other and much more differentiated and internalised understanding of boundaries amongst in-group members. Even though I was able to squeeze cultural Web pages into a defined box that could be closed and marked with a cultural genre label, such a method would ignore the diversity of Web pages and Inuit, as well as the subtle way in which identity is expressed on Web pages – some of which might have no more than an Inukshuk on their front page, a piece of syllabic text or a word about the local community. This book should be regarded as a study of social relations in the lines of social constructions rather than a study on characterisation.

Wanted: Practical Method

Cyberspace is not more complex than physical space and nor are the methodological considerations that need to be addressed perplexing beyond reality. If arguing the opposite – that a differentiation is necessary in the overall basic rules of fieldwork in cyberspace versus physical space – one would vividly have to ignore what Thomas points out: that it would mean ignoring every situation as unique, thus breeding a "litany of rules" (1996); a new method and rule to every situation. My methods are, at the most, slightly different than those of usual Arctic anthropology because of the type of space they are applied to. But at the end of the day my methods address the same world. The use of information technology for fieldwork should not be confused with a metaphor for an objectification of research, nor does the physical distance engendered by this type of communication suggest an increased dependency on judgements or estimates on behalf of the researcher. These elements have more to do with the choices of the individual researcher, rather than being characteristics of an absolute methodology for online fieldwork. One should acknowledge the possibility that "the methodology, though purportedly neutral, incorporates a particular account of selfhood and masquerades it as a universal concept" (Powell 1997:14). Indeed, I accept that my research is subjective in many ways: if not would not have put my name to it, although it deals with other people rather than myself.

No matter how many examples I give of different Web pages and diversity in cultural identity as well as social boundaries, they would never match the diversity found amongst Inuit themselves. Inuit by far are defined and define themselves by their social organisation in physical/offline space rather than online. The amount of physical references in text, pictures, maps and photographs on Inuit Web pages affirms this. As I have found, stereotypes are used to a great extent in getting the attention of visitors, and this blurs much of the differentiation that actually exists offline amongst Inuit.

To get around a stereotyped Inuit image in Web content, it is necessary to break out of the centripetal cyber paradigm and include physicality in analysis: i.e. particularise the geographic and social differences that actually exist and by which Inuit organise their lives. Hence, I try to provide the reader with a diverse understanding of Inuit in cyberspace and among other things show that Inuit might be proud of their heritage, but not bound to the TimeSpace of their ancestors, nor especially bewildered in the age of postmodern alienation/fragmentation because of non-space. Cyberspace does not make Inuit any less Inuit, as was pointed out in the introduction, and thus Inuit in cyberspace is not a quest for romanticising or sensationalising the life of Inuit as much as it is an ordinary anthropological study on the use of a new space for communication and representation. I must emphasise that my rather extensive use of Internet communication does not originate from a techno-centric mind, as much as I believe it comes from an experimenting and practical one.

II

(Re)producing the Arctic in Cyberspace

More than 300 very different Web sites have been browsed during my research. Not all pages are made by Inuit, but by others who live in the Arctic as well. Most of the Web pages, nevertheless, address the world Inuit live in and often make direct reference to Inuit. Yet, in contrast to the singularity suggested by the title of this book, *Inuit in Cyberspace*, the Web pages often display an immense diversity within the Arctic and amongst the Inuit: local entities such as Adam Grim from Aappilattoq, Greenland, the Inuvialuit in Inuvik, the Yup'ik of Alaska or the Inuit Circumpolar Conference. So among the many socio-physical entities, it is very important to notice the broad range of physical, personal, social and cultural diversity to be found both online as well as offline. Many of the Web pages are constructed so to assert different levels of space for a given group or individual within a community in a specific physical location, region, etc – a space that often ends up as somehow typically peripheral in regard to a larger entity in a social as well as physical dimension.

Pickard, in her study on the construction of community in cyberspace (1998), calls the World Wide Web a 'social landscape' amongst other landscapes such as e-mail and IRC. In another case, Nuttall finds that Inuit in the small village of Kangersuatsiaq, Greenland, create a 'memoryscape' – a mental image of the landscape where remembrance of places as well as their local names denotes community. "All give a sense of a bounded locality distinct from the memoryscape of neighbouring communities" (1992:3). Therefore, while peripherality as a notion of specific locality is often a common denominator on many Web pages, the peripheral reference is relative to the size of locality. The many different dimensions of 'community' and local identity that can be found embedded on Web pages make it difficult to talk about a certain 'Inuit' identity, in so far as I should be talking about several local identities or modes of identification – some of which may seem more localised or cultural than others, depending on their content or purpose. The multitude of communities and social boundaries that a Web master constructs into a Web page function, in a reflection of the point to Cohen's discussion on the construction of symbolic community, as "a resource and repository of meaning, and a referent of their identity" (1985:118). In this sense, some Web pages, such as some Greenlandic ones, are constructed to situate themselves in a social and physical (socio-physical) space that is local within the national perspective, while others locate themselves within the Arctic, and others again locate themselves within the World. Mostly, however, the Web pages are constructed to locate themselves within several or all of the above mentioned frameworks, portraying the social interaction of Web masters at global, regional as well as a local levels.

Thus, Eric Anoee locates himself in his Web pages[32] of by referring to his family, work, the community of Arviat and Nunavut. He links to other Web pages of regional ISPs, schools in Nunavut and a wide array of Nunavut Boards, Nunatisaq News (Nunavut online newspaper) as well as News North. As a result, the socio-physical periphery is automatically contextualised in relation to the worldwide network of other users and their different backgrounds and locations. Although his location is a centre of attention in the time frame of each user's visit, it is peripheral within the locations of other users and for the numbers of other users that he presents himself to.

In her discussion of 'place' as underlying the social organisation and cultural identities of local communities in Greenland, Dybbroe states that: "local identity is a symbolic construction, where (the fact of) peripherality in the objective world informs the sense of belonging and identity. Peripherality is not just a political reality, but becomes a state of mind" (1991:5). By linking to other Web pages that relate to the Arctic or a region on a supra-level, or by linking to many local pages, Web masters construct what is simultaneously periphery and centre. Thus, it seems that many Arctic Web pages that address locality, community or cultural identity stress the position of peripherality to help create an even stronger sense of belonging – or not belonging as it would be in regard to out-group members. In either case, the strategy is likely to attract both in-group as well as out-group members: in-group members because they feel somehow at home and out-group members because they feel attracted to the space that is exotic and foreign. So while it is often heard that the Internet compresses the feeling of physical distance, these Web pages, nevertheless, use the sensation to assert a distance to the rest of the world by referring to socio-physical boundaries that are limited in size. This creates a sense of belonging that is more culturally localised than merely being one of hundreds of millions of users on the Internet. As Dybbroe concludes after having found that the cultural policies of Greenland embed historical differences of locals rather than a collective national future (1991:15), "despite mobility of residence you always come from a place": a place or a space, I should add, that is constructed not only by physical means but by social means as well. Yet, in the perspectives of visionaries, cyberspace is seen as a new global *Gemeinschaft*[33], supposedly bringing together individuals who, instead of their constrained participation in *Gesellschafts* (associations) of modern time, now seek 'Post-Enlightenment' in the unconstrained space. Locality in physical space supposedly looses power as a centre of social meaning to the gain of *deterritorialised* relationships. In contrast, the cultural representation of Inuit on the Web questions whether the effect of advanced communication is that clear-cut.

The myth of cyberspace

The ideological outsets for cyberspace created and locomoted, among others, by Gibson (1984) and Barlow (1996) have been developed into a combined manifest of cyberspace as a *non-space*, a space without boundaries, of unthinkable complexity and with few or no cultural differences. An immortal space of impunity where no one is hungry and everybody is equal, where there are no human bodies or physical restrictions – in other words a utopian safe haven. This is a space where Barlow holds that there is no matter, as a result of which, here, matter is also without meaning. The boundaries of class, nation, ethnic identity, religion, geography, language, gender and more are said to be transcendent in cyberspace, i.e. they evade the eye and our attention – a fathom that is generally embraced by enthusiasts because of its unlimited opportunities within a broad range of psychological, social, political and economical dimensions.

While not all enthusiasts agree on the importance and possibilities of transcendence, they see the development of the Internet as positive[34], while some of these see cyberspace as a place to create new identities that are liberated from the constraints of physical life[35]. Under this optic, cultural identities are not really regarded as being immobile, but there seems to be little interest in developing ideas about the assertion of already existing cultural identities in cyberspace, as much as there is an immense interest in the creation of new cybercultural identities – non-space identities that are not vested in a physical world, but which allow their bearers to shift between a multitude of unconstrained and self-chosen "selves". Cyberspace is transformed into the place of unlimited potential and possibility in contrast to the physical world where people are constrained by power, physicality, economy and culture. While the matters of culture and place may still have meaning in cyberspace, it is only in a new construction of their meanings that they have any user potential.

Thus cultures, such as Inuit cultures, supposedly exist in a world that is limited compared to that of new cybercultures. Those Inuit Web users who do exist run the risk – or have the chance, as others would say – of cutting themselves off from the social space of their communities. Yet, where much socialising online potentially diminishes the time a person can spend on such activities offline, ethnic or cultural identity is not necessarily affected by this. In regard to modernisation and ethnic identity in Greenland, Kleivan finds that in contrast to the theory of acculturation, where the educated segment is supposedly more likely to shift identity than those who pursue more traditional/cultural occupations, individuals moving to the milieu of 'the other' do not cast away their group membership as much as follow some personal aspiration. In conclusion, "differences in aspirations are no proof of differences in ethnic identification" (1969/70:211). The same, I find, goes for Inuit Web users who interact in cyberspace.

Critics of utopians differ in their approaches to the phenomenon of cyberspace[36]. Some, like Postman, have a greater interest in the suppose decline of culture because of technology. Technopoly, Postman's idea of a totalitarian technocracy, makes alternatives to itself invisible (transcendent) and redefines what we understand by family, religion, politics, truth, history, privacy and intelligence. Technopoly redefines our world so it fits its own requirements. His solution recommends that we go back to basics and bring "a halt to the thrust of a technological thought-world" (1993:199) – mainly through education. However, sympathetic as Postman's ideas may seem, they appear to walk the corridors of futurist visions and rather than engaging utopians in everyday practicality – an area they mostly deal with in futurist scenarios – he adopts their futurist rhetoric in his own work.

Differently, Robins is engaged in questioning the mythical dreamworld of virtual reality and transcendence: how to bring the 'real' world into the discussion. He finds that the focus on disembodiment amongst utopian theorists has created a myth of cyberspace where it seems as if "social and political turbulence of our time – ethnic conflict, resurgent nationalism, urban fragmentation – had nothing at all to do with virtual space" (1995:137). The world has been extrapolated into two different worlds, offline versus online. For this reason, my approach is along the lines of Robins when he recommends that "it is time that this real world broke in on the virtual one" (ibid:137): a thread that has also been taken up by Lillie in his thesis on cultural uses of ICTs and their implications for Latino identities, where he investigates how cultural identities are maintained in a changing world (1998). Mitra describes excellently how a specific Web site functions as a meeting place for diasporic Indians as well as a place where culture and social organisation are negotiated with out-group Web users who also use the site (1997).

It is noted that a response to the latest development, where the world is breaking in on cyberspace, is somehow paradoxical as many utopians now pledge allegiance to a more or less 'Habermasian contest' to argue that only the former text-written environments uphold the real democratic potential, while the new commercialised developments are somehow deviant in those concerns (Loader 1997:11). As maintained in the discussions here, the development of the Web, commercialised or not, has opened opportunities to other than privileged urban pioneers who are fluent in English.

The transcendent or hallucinatory notion clearly emerged in the early days when the Internet was mostly the privilege of people within Euro-American society. As the Internet grows, including or excluding people from other cultures and areas, transcendence seems to have flourished beyond its own invisible capabilities in many respects. I find, however, that in many ways the transcendent conception of cyberspace matches the use of the exciting and captivating fantasy worlds of MUD or MOO but, even then, vividly disregards the fact that it all takes place in the same world – a world consisting of many subordinates, where cyberspace could be one of them. People use these portals for the process of building networks and exchanging information and meaning: they do not live in computers but use them to engage with the world.

In the respective minds of pessimists and optimists, often polarised in opinion as they are, the idea of cyberspace seems to be treated as the mother of all good or all bad. All the stuff in between, used by people on a daily basis to basically live their lives, seems to be extrapolated out of context to the point where all-encompassing ideology starts and mediating practicality ceases. Hamelink concludes in the development perspective of a United Nations discussion paper that: "relying upon utopian or dystopian perspectives, the debate will get stuck between the empirical evidence that automation eliminates jobs ... [a]nd the evidence that automation creates new jobs" (1997:30). So although this split-world notion seems to be on retreat in research, it still pervades the abundance of media hype dealing with the Internet. I will approach the theme within the lines of a practicality that investigates how Inuit Web users use online cyberspace to have offline consequences. Now please consider the two following paragraphs:

> "Cyberspace. A consensual hallucination experienced daily by billions of legitimate operators, in every nation ... A graphic representation of data abstracted from the banks of every computer in the human system. Unthinkable complexity. Lines of light ranged in the nonspace of the mind, clusters and constellations of data. Like city lights, receding ..." (Gibson 1984 [1995]:67).

> "… I showed my dad, who is [age]³⁷ years of age, and just to see what it really does, I had a letter sent on the e-mail to my [relative] in [location], where he took part in the main message and she responded back the next day and I showed my dad when he came back to see what kind of response my [relative] gave and he said that, when we were in residential school, it used to take 2 to 3 months to just get a response to a mail from us and he said that, this should have been around then, then we wouldn't have missed each other so much if daily contact was maintained through this new medium and it probably would have saved us from losing our language, which we had to regain in our adult life today. And I think he was right, if we had a continuing dialogue with our parents this way, we would not have lost touch with our parents." Male, Cambridge Bay, Nunavut, Canada (personal communication, 1998).

Undeniably, this is set up a little prejudiced, but it is clear that one is more abstract than the other. Although neither of the two paragraphs address the use of Web pages directly, the first paragraph, a quite famous and decidedly used one, outlines an abstract ideological notion of cyberspace[38], while the second paragraph outlines the everyday practicality of cyberspace. It is my intention to centre discussions around the practicalities of the latter, rather than the abstractions of the former. As part of a critique on the 'consensual hallucination' of cyberspace, Robins coins it when noticing that "the mythology of Cyberspace is preferred over its sociology" (1995:153). A point of view that seems similar to that of Kawagley's Yupiaq view on western technology: "The syncopating strobe lights have been transformed into a myth, a religious play, and we faithfully accept these gods of the new world" (Kawagley 1995:110). Following their perspectives I shall attempt to demythicise cyberspace in an Arctic perspective.

On the Web, it seems as if all the distinguishing boundaries that disregard the notion of non-space are the rule rather than the exception. Here, Inuit and others continue referring to ethnic, geographic, linguistic and national boundaries in their attempts to configure the sensation of space as they know it – socially, mentally, culturally and geographically. Doing this, they (re)produce, reflect and assert much of what they know already: their reference to social and physical space renders concomitant continuity between offline and online identity, rather than being confinements of online identity only. Indeed, as I shall discuss later, this is affirmed, too, when other people access their Web pages. Both parties point to cultural identity, religious beliefs, locations in physical space and, in addition, Inuit strategically use their languages on parts of the Web to affirm boundaries and identity: for example in guestbooks, where people display ethnic affiliation, kinship, their geographic location and language as some of the most common ways of presenting themselves.

One might ask whether or not utopian transcendence can be evident. The use of e-mail and text-written environments seem to promote the sensation of non-space transcendence, but the Web with its many reflections from offline life does not currently fit the more Gibsonian notion of cyberspace. Needless to say, the notion of transcendence – novel, chivalrous or gracious as it may be – is not one corresponding to the entire use of the Internet. In the case of the Inuit, that use currently includes both cyberspace and physical space, no matter how much some people attempt to run a mental divide through the social and mental space bridging the two, either by glorifying or identifying the phenomenon as another Mephistopheles. This study does not question whether some Inuit agree with utopian or dystopian approaches to ICTs or not. But, either way, the use of the Internet by some Inuit some of the time opposes the transcendent notion of cyberspace.

Peripherality on the Net

Let the discussion above serve as a vantage point for the more narrow analysis of Web pages in chapter four and instead be exceeded now by the idea of peripherality and the Internet. I am often confronted with the idea that cyberspace renders its users free from the physical constraints of being contained in a body – the state of mind is called disembodiment. However, peoples' use of the Internet does not only conform to their disembodied actions online, but are very much affected by their offline embodiment as well – at least in the Arctic.

I will try to give a basic, overall view of different incentives in regard to Internet communication policies in the Canadian Arctic, Greenland and Alaska, as well as in the rural or peripheral reality that these technologies and people exist within. On an overall basis, it will merely give the reader some different perspectives on the world outside cyberspace, what kind of obstacles Inuit face offline and, among other things, illustrate that cyberspace is not always about endless hours of surfing the Web, conducting e-commerce or building cybercommunities in hallucinatory spaces, but very much about remembering physicality and facts such as living in the Arctic where 500 miles or more of long distance dial up to reach a server is far from unusual and usually expensive. It will show that there is a connection between the physicality that I have found embedded on Web pages and the physical reality of the Arctic where Inuit live.

"Building network is a piece of cake ... putting people together to use it is difficult" (Pena, Technical Support Manager, Mexico - personal communication between Pena and Richardson in Richardson 1996:4). People in rural[39] or peripheral areas around the world are foretold many advantages by accessing the Internet. Featherstone and Burrows, along the lines of the cyberpunk genre, explain cyberspace as an urban environment like Le Corbusier's Metropolis, where no one can really get an overall view of the plan from above but have to move about on the ground and experience it (1995:11). Similarly, Gibson writes "Lines of light ranged *in the nonspace of the mind*, clusters and constellations of data. *Like city lights*, receding ..." (1984:67, my italics). The speed of exchanging information and the promoted feeling of physical proximity is said to attach these more and less peripheral and isolated areas more closely to the power centres of economy, politics, education, administration and services: among other things, making medical services better, enhancing the administrative relation between governmental administration and citizen and creating economic potential for the small and medium-sized businesses (SMEs) existing in these areas[40]. Overall, these measures will alter differences across geographical, cultural, economic, social and political borders and help Inuit escape the marginalisation of their peripheral position on the global scene.

But as mentioned earlier in the introductory chapter, this line of argumentation sometimes helps to produce a split image of the world where cyberspace solves problems or enables opportunities that are almost out of this world. From a pessimistic point of view, one notices how people seem to forget that while peripheral rural areas may very well attain these opportunities, the centres of power and accumulation are just as likely to benefit from even better services and opportunities. As argued by Bollman "... if space still has a price or where space still has a price, rurality exists" (1994:141). Hence, it does not come as a surprise that the geographical representation of participants in my own fieldwork suggests that Inuit in bigger towns have better accessibility to the Internet than those living in remoter and smaller villages.

So it is important to stress that the use of the technology cannot automatically be expected to change existing power structures, whether these are economic, social or political, but can very well help the peripheral areas from being further marginalised. Bauman holds in regard to the consequences of this globalising phenomena that power has become weightless (1998:19) but nevertheless is still dominated by an elite. In regard to ICTs as the solution to economic problems of rural areas, it is an idea characterised by "some degree of wishful thinking" (Gurstein 1998: paragraph 38). I might add, that the same applies to other socio-political features as well.

Peripheral and isolated areas, such as the Arctic, do not necessarily represent major problems in establishing the technology locally. What often makes the establishment of networks costly or difficult in these areas is to a large extent the linkage out from the remote areas and the limited numbers of users who are to pay for this – thus an economic and political rather than a technological problem. However, as suggested by Pedersen in regard to Greenlandic users, economic considerations, in terms of the price of access, may not always represent the most important obstacle for them in comparison with entire IT costs (1998: 228). To illustrate, the lack of physical infrastructure connecting these areas presents economic obstacles for establishing a cost-efficient communications infrastructure, as there are few intermediaries en route that contribute to the network and essentially cut costs. This again complicates the large scale establishment of local networks, connected within the regional and national infrastructure. It is precisely the infrastructures that urban areas have which rural areas in the Arctic lack. Yet, one should note that there are urban settings within the rural Arctic, making the differentiation between rural and urban concepts fuzzy. Still, the regions that have an edge in these investments are often located outside the Arctic. As an example, in 1998, CAD 120 million were invested in a Canadian initiative to develop a faster optical network under the title CA*net 3. This enables speeds that are up to 1.5 million times faster than a standard 28.8 kbp modem on the ordinary telephone networks. This is a follow-up on CA*net II, a network finished last year, crossing Canada from Newfoundland to British Columbia, thus avoiding the Arctic regions of Canada[41]. Still, as I shall show in the sections about Alaska, Canada and Greenland, this does not necessarily mean that the Arctic falls behind in the technological hyper race.

Clicking on a hyperlink, for example, from the directory Web page of the Arctic Slope Regional Corporation (ASRC)[42] in Barrow, Alaska, will take me directly to their subsidiary, Arctic Slope World Services[43], in Sacramento, California, just as easily as if I was to choose a company in Barrow itself, such as the Arctic Slope Native Association[44]. In other words, the physical distance seems levelled out and one might ask what this does to the notion of rurality. As something of a paradox, the information provided on many Inuit Web pages asserts the sense of distances to peripherality in a medium that is characterised, in the cyberpunk genre, by its urban settings. While deterritorialising themselves by representation through a medium that is said to shift the paradigm of culture as being congruent with a specific space beyond theoretical doubt, they simultaneously reterritorialise themselves in this new space by reasserting and defining boundaries consistent with offline space; displaying images of the Arctic nature, its animals, pinpointing their geographical positions on maps and more.

Since much research is currently undertaken to understand the effects of the Internet amongst rural[45] and marginalised populations in the quest to limit hardship due to physical distance and isolation, I shall briefly touch upon some aspects with relevance to the concept of rurality and place. In retrospect, my fieldwork did not introduce the concept of rurality in discussions and interviews with participants. Yet, the discussions often circled around topics that engaged with many different connotations of the same word: being isolated, peripherality, Inuit ways of living and more.

Shucksmith discusses rurality as a social concept (1994). My conception rests between the more physical notion of rurality and a social one. However, the sense of rurality, reflected through much of the information published on Inuit Web pages, is often an explicit reflection of how people live in physical space and one notes dynamic relations between sociality and physicality: how people bind their identity to what it means to live in isolated Arctic communities. The dynamics between memoryscape/landscape (Nuttall 1992), meaning of place (Dybbroe 1991), the symbolic construction of community and identity (Cohen 1985) and social organisation (Barth 1969) are expressed vividly on Web pages – and I will discuss those perspectives further in the next chapter. But significantly, the sense of rurality/peripherality, both socially and physically, is important in the processes of asserting cultural identity on many Inuit Web pages.

Many Inuit Web users that I corresponded with during fieldwork made reference to the ease and speed of sending and receiving e-mail, documents and accessing resources through the Internet, compared to earlier, but continued to express the dichotomy between their possibilities from the periphery compared to those empowered urban population centres, both implicitly and explicitly:

> "... Not the least, it's also a nice thing [online shopping], that all different types of merchandise can be examined and ordered through the Internet, again even if you live here where the choice of goods is very limited." Male, Ammassalik, Greenland (as translated by author from Danish to English, personal communication, 1998).

> "We live in an isolated town. The airplane ticket to go anywhere is very expensive. We are hope [sic] the Internet will bring long distance education for student research and long

distance communication for both individuals and business/corporations/associations, etc." Female, Rankin Inlet, Nunavut, Canada (personal communication, 1998).

Pahl (1965) argues that early community studies created a simplistic division between urban and rural, and notes that one finds places in rural settings that are still part of the urban system, as well as urban communities that are considered rural: in other words, that the distinction of Toennies' (1957 [1887]) 'Gemeinschaft' (community) and 'Gesellschaft' (association) simply could not differentiate appropriately between the social organisation of rural and urban communities. With the introduction of the Internet, this grey zone of terms seems to have become wider. While many Inuit Web pages refer to entities of local community, they assert this within global dimensions. The distinction of local communities on Web pages does not characterise the Web masters as members of self-contained communities, as much as it depicts them as active agents who express locality in a diverse network of social organisation beyond the local dimension – using the local as a platform for self-representation. Inuit often self-image themselves as part of isolated communities or regions but do this in an arena that is global. While Pahl found the divide to be simplistic, and I agree, many Web users, nevertheless, express the peripheral/centre divide as a token of importance and difference. The feeling of isolation and peripherality is part of their different cultural identities – even though they have the Internet.

On user levels, the Internet is often discussed in terms of the ease of ordering merchandise on the Internet from around the globe, such as clothes, equipment, music, books and the ease of interacting with others outside the Arctic region. But the peripheral feeling is closely linked to Inuit sociality. The technological potential entices the Web masters to bring their rural sociality and reality closer to other people, through maps, photographs, sounds and text, promoting the sensation of proximity on an interacting level, but manifesting the difference that is needed for the assertion of place and identity.

Three regions:
Canadian Arctic, Greenland and Alaska

In a 1994 symposium arranged by the Inuit Broadcasting Company, the Government of the North West Territories and Inuit Communications Systems Limited, both Inuit and others formed discussion groups in 27 communities. They listened to panel discussions and gave feedback via an impressive network of satellites and telephone lines while using videoconferences, live and taped TV, telefax, Asynchronous Transfer Mode and computers – even an Australian audience participated. The objective was to let existing and potential users help define how and why the North should be connected to the growing global communication networks. The discussions during the symposium's three days addressed the issues of cost-efficient and equal access, the impact on culture and language, the need for training to design and use the Internet, accountability in use and maintenance, the need for Northern participation in research and development and, not least, how to fund development (Inuit Broadcasting Company 1994). Many things were said and done. However, as the symposium ended, much of the technology was removed and many smaller settlements were again left with the few phone-lines they previously had.

In 1998, four years later, ARDICOM[46], a corporation entirely owned by Northern companies, 66% of which are owned by aboriginal interests, completed its goal – to connect 58 communities in the Canadian North, from a commissioned by the GNWT. Although all these communities are now potentially supplied with a network connection, only the 11 largest communities can attract ISPs (Internet Service Providers). However, some of the ISPs not only fear that ARDICOM might eventually turn into an ISP – although ARDICOM maintains again and again that it will not – but these ISPs further suggest that they can do it cheaper than ARDICOM, and would thus invest in their own satellite links without the use of ARDICOM's network. For example, Cascade Publications/Inuvik TV in Inuvik, a large community of some 3,300 residents in the Mackenzie Delta of Canada, funded its own satellite link at the price of USD 100,000 with six times the bandwidth of ARDICOM's network by using the community cable network (NEWS/NORTH 1997:A22; Zellen 1998:paragraph 30). Actually, Inuvik TV was the first company in Canada to hook up to the network through a high-speed satellite link (Stryde 1997).

Four ISPs – SSI Micro, Nunanet Worldwide Communications Ltd, Sakku Arctic Technologies and Polarnet – joined a partnership in 1999 by the name of Arctic Logic to ensure what they call "a partnership for the next millennium"[47]. However at the moment, the smaller and more peripheral settlements without enough customers, and therefore potential customers for local ISPs, are still the ones being left behind in the standard of accessibility. Even though the network is practically on people's doorstep because of ARDICOM, the residents of peripheral communities have no choice but to dial-up long distance to reach servers of ISPs in the larger communities. As an example Nunanet Communications with some 900 customers in 1998 is the only ISP on Baffin Island within 1,000 miles of Iqaluit, the capital of Nunavut, to service potential customers (De Santis 1998). Despite the potentials for residents of peripheral communities, it seems quite clear that those who do not live close to an ISP are at a disadvantage in their use of the medium if they need to access through long-distance calling. It is therefore clear that the World Science Report of UNESCO is right when pointing out that ICTs used in a wrong way may just as well reinforce the potential social risk (1996:273). In similar vein, the Inuit Circumpolar Conference stated, as early as 1992, that "the collective and individual right to communicate is increasingly viewed as a new emerging human right" (1992:107). The imbalance in regard to the cost of access and service, however, may be somewhat changed with the introduction of free competition on long-distance calling, but it is very unlikely to disappear.

After July 1, 2000, competition was opened for other phone companies to compete with companies like Northwestel as long-distance providers (Wilkin 1998): much the same as what happened in Alaska with the Telecommunication Act of 1996 in regard to competition. Northwestel, the network operator of the North West Territories, Yukon, Nunavut and part of British Columbia have requested a subsidy of CAD 20 to 30 million to handle the situation. They claim that as much as 90% of the communities they serve produce a loss despite the expensive rates (Wilkin 1998) basically because 80% of the communities they serve have less than 500 customers (Northwestel 1998: paragraph 26), which pushes their operating cost to twice the amount per customer compared to Bell Canada (bid: paragraph 37). Similar to the case of free competition on long-distance calling in Alaska, cheaper long-distance rates and more expensive local rates are likely to be the outcome. While this will lower the price of access for users who live distant from local/regional ISPs, it is likely to make it harder for local ISPs, since other ISPs down south can start to compete at cheap long-distance rates.

Amongst other initiatives in Canada affecting the Inuit was the Nunavik Net in northern Quebec. It was launched in August 1996 by Inuit-owned production and broadcasting company Taqramiut Nipingat Inc. (TNI), together with a selection of partners, including the Community Access Programme[48] (CAP). However, the entire project collapsed after just about one year, in 1997, when TNI could no longer pay the long distance phone bills to reach the ISP. At this point TNI was footing a bill for three free access centres at the price of approximately CAD 10,000 a piece per month. Consequently it was arranged in such a way that the users themselves were to pay for their online time via telephone credit cards, but this had no effect as the server, located in distant Montreal, was connected through a satellite link, thus making dial-up connection rather expensive. After the project was abandoned, the costs continued to haunt the budgets of TNI for a couple of years – the cost of investments and satellite use combined reached as much CAD 630,000. Regional Makivik Corporation was involved as well and lost as much as CAD 750,000 through the bankruptcy of its subsidiary Unaaq, the Montreal based consultancy firm who first proposed the network to TNI.

Another initiative is SchoolNet[49]; established in 1993 as part of an international scheme, that has ensured all Canadian schools the opportunity of connecting to the network by March 31, 1999. This initiative has been supported by a great number of tele-companies, educational associations, provincial ministries of education, first nations and many more on a national level. Networked learning and tele-medicine are increasingly being used – not only in the Canadian Arctic but in Greenland and Alaska as well.

Another initiative comes from Nortext[50], who own the bilingual online newspaper Nunatsiaq News. As Inuktitut syllabics have become part of Unicode that allows the characters to be recognised by computers worldwide (Thomas 1998), Nortext has produced the Nunavut

Handbook[51] (a travel-guide) and developed the nunacom font for computers that is downloadable from the bilingual Nunavut.com[52] Web site. The Web site has turned into a large resource on Nunavut Web sites, as well as functioned as the initial test site for the implementation of syllabic characters on the Web.

Being the first country in the world after Iceland to have a fully digital communications network in late 1996[53], Greenland is focused on maintaining a modern telecommunications network and using it. This is highlighted in three comprehensive reports on IT policies from 1996, 1997 and 2000, where all possible aspects of how to use IT to develop the country further economically, democratically, politically, educationally and socially are analysed and discussed thoroughly (Grønlands Hjemmestyre [Greenland Home Rule] 1996, 1997, Grønlands IT-Råd [IT Council of Greenland] 2000). As in other parts of the Arctic, or other parts of the world for that matter, discussions in Greenland about the Internet are a recurrent part of public and political debate and seem focused upon Greenland's potentials as an information society where everybody will have equal access to a vast amount of governmental and political information, wherein tele-medicine and long-distance education or e-commerce are ordinary elements of society rather than pilot projects.

However, 1999 witnessed that Ilisimatusarfik, the University in Nuuk, with some 100 students, only had access to five student computers, of which two did not function properly. As a result the national IT council asked Greenlandic businesses to sponsor the University with computers. At the time conditions seemed different at the Business College (NiuernermikIlinniarfik) in Nuuk where 60 students had access to 45 computers while, at the Journalist College, each student had access to a computer (Grønlands Radioavis [KNR Radio News] 1999a). Thus, there is not only a large difference in accessibility on a national level between small settlements and larger towns, but also amongst the different institutions of higher education in Nuuk as well. While the national IT strategies aim at connectivity across villages and towns, it is currently the people in larger towns that primarily experience the blessings and problems of computerisation.

Tele Greenland[54], the national network operator, is renowned for its know-how on telecommunications in rural and challenging environments, as well as providing consultancy abroad. Ever since the Internet was made commonly available all over the country, in 1996, the corporation has maintained its status as a monopoly being the only ISP, asserting what is almost a tradition of Greenlandic monopolies. Having the position as the network operator, they can offer the Internet as a special service whereby they cut off any private ISPs from entering the market, which in 1999 consisted of at least 2,300 users who connected via a modem – not counting ISDN users at large businesses and governmental institutions (Hansen 1999:9). It is this combination of being both a network operator and an ISP that the ISPs in the Canadian Arctic fear. In Greenland Internet users pay a nationwide minute rate and do not have to worry about long distance charges to reach the servers of larger communities. The minute price in 1999 for Internet access was approximately DKK 10,000 (approximately USD 1,500) for 200 hours of Internet use. However, Tele Greenland is considering a new method of payment, where the users pay for the amount of data they send and retrieve. This would make it free to view Web pages once they are downloaded and users would only have to pay for the size of data transmission. It is still too soon to tell when or whether this sort of system will be implemented (Grønlands Radioavis [KNR Radio News] 1999b). However, small settlements generally have a limited amount of connections available per person compared to bigger communities that also have faster network connections and better services – a common phenomenon throughout the Arctic and the rest of the world.

KNI Pilersuisoq[55], the Greenlandic shipping division, started a pilot project to establish the world's northernmost Internet café, in Innaarsuit. In Hansen's status report on the first year of the Net café, he concludes that the residents of Innaarsuit seem ready to use the Internet, while external contributors such as government institutions or the media, such as newspapers, seem less inclined to provide the input that the villagers are waiting for: or are simply not yet ready to do so. Thus, villagers have few visions of what the Internet could be used for in the future, beyond what it is already used for today (Hansen 1999:64). Today, the Innaarsuit café project has basically stopped, but two other privately run internet cafés now exist in Nuuk and Sisimiut.

Another part of the KNI strategy (Lauritsen 1998) is to link all their stores along the coast to a central network, where the store managers order their goods electronically from the central warehouses. The next question here seems to be whether or not to skip the store manager and offer the opportunity for customers to order goods directly, as it is normally done on the Web. As competition moves in with online stores such as the Canadian based Qamutit Express[56], KNI will probably need to develop a more explicit strategy.

The telecommunications policies of Alaska are characterised by liberalistic policies that are less visible in the Canadian Arctic and even less, if at all, existent in Greenland, as the following statement suggests: "Market economics will guide the provision of telecommunications services throughout the state unless there is a compelling public interest served by direct State intervention to insure the safety and well-being of its citizens" (Telecommunication Information Council 1996). There are several small local ISPs in Alaska, especially in the south and southeast, as well as some larger companies like Internet Alaska[57] or GCI who have their own networks. Up north, in Barrow, the local cable company provides Internet services through their TV cable network.

In 1999, GCI, a major telecom company, advertised free Internet services to all its long-distance customers in Alaska. As a peculiarity of tele-infrastructure in Alaska, it is sometimes cheaper dialling long-distance servers in the lower 48 than state-wide if one lives in a small community with no ISP; simply because of the free competition on long-distance calls. GCI who hold roughly 40% of the long-distance phone market in Alaska completed a USD 125 million project establishing a fibre optic cable running from Seattle to Anchorage. To cover their expenses they wanted access to some of the estimated 73,000 internet users in Alaska of whom Internet Alaska, the largest ISP in Alaska, claims to have 30,000. Smaller and local ISPs were not late to point out the danger of a monopoly arising, however, so far no legal action has been taken (Sprenger 1999). In addition, three native corporations, Arctic Slope Regional Corporation (ASRC), Ahtna Incorporated and Chugach Alaska Corporation joined into partnership with Kanas Telecom Inc. together with MFS Communications Company and won a contract for the construction of an 800-mile fibre optic line between

Prudhoe Bay and Valdez following the already existing Trans-Alaska Pipeline. The system was ordered by the Alyeska Pipeline Service Company[58] who now use it for surveying their pipeline as well as corresponding between offices and facilities. As an extra, it is also used by all the communities in between (TundraTimes 1996:5).

Very much like the Canadian SchoolNet, the Alaska Science and Technology Foundation awarded USD 10,000 to each Alaskan public school to wire their classrooms[59] (TundraTimes 1997:1, 5). As an extra help, BP (British Petroleum) donated some 1,500 computers to schools throughout the state's 15 school districts. Other corporations, such as GCI and Apple Computers also contributed to the programme. The northernmost and largest school district in the US, North Slope Borough School District[60], has ensured the network access of its ten schools in eight communities.

Already in 1995 a network by the name of the "Community Health Aid Information Network" was ready for use linking 15 local clinics to the Norton Sound Health Corporation (NSHC) and Norton Sound Regional Hospital. The network allows for the transfer of e-mails with the attachment of photographs, sounds and picture clips from camcorders, much like other tele-medicine initiatives such as in Canada and Greenland.

Bridging a gap?

As suggested earlier in this chapter, building networks is easier than getting people to use them. Therefore one should be wary of being solely focused on establishing the fastest or newest technology to process economy, politics, education and social life. However, the Arctic, with its vast distances and low population density, is a near ideal place to make this sort of technology work – interconnecting people across vast distances. According to the material gathered during my online fieldwork, the majority of participants believed that the societal development was closely linked with the development of this technology and its future use. In conclusion the effects that small rural communities are hoped to experience seem relative since these peripheral communities are almost as a rule the last to be served. Instead of "bridging the gap", it seems as if the residents in these small communities can merely try to prevent the gap from becoming wider. The supposed democratic, economic and social effect of roaming cyberspace are highly relative: basically, the effect seems mostly directed at those fortunate enough to already be reasonably connected. During the first part of fieldwork I experienced requests by some Canadian Inuit to get questionnaires e-mailed to them, because their Internet connections were too slow and expensive for them to access the questionnaire on the Web.

Still, it has been and still is maintained by advisory bodies that the Internet provides the chance for rural or peripheral communities to "bridge the gap" between the 'haves' and 'have nots'[61]. This seemingly avoids the fact that the subject becomes ambivalent when I find some rural communities within rural areas of the Arctic are more rural, or else more urban, than others. These seem to be notions that peripheral Internet development planning has a tendency to ignore or forget. No matter how much the Arctic is wired, establishment and maintenance cost are often likely to go higher and bounce back on the customer or the entrepreneur, impeding or at least placing a sanction on their use of the medium, compared to conditions in the South.

III

A Common Web of Difference and Similarity

By exploring Inuit Web pages on the Internet I will address how offline cultural, personal and local identities are constructed, negotiated and identified in cyberspace: specifically how aspects of Inuit culture, social organisation and identity are asserted by communicating those social and physical boundaries of the world that some refer to as 'real'. In contrast to the argument that people's use of cyberspace dissolves boundaries, its use can also maintain or construct boundaries. I have found many Inuit and Arctic Web pages to mirror such a reality. The pages may depict physical maps of land claim areas that Inuit negotiators have struggled for in decades; photographs of Inuit in the Arctic environment; paintings, stone carvings and prints made by Inuit artists; aerial photos of physical communities with roads, oil tanks, trucks, antennas and satellite dishes – the realities of personal selves as well as group identities. Put bluntly, they visualise a space that is not transcendent but which nevertheless is still able to be dynamically asserted in both cyberspace as well as physical space. They visualise and explain the world they live in.

These Web pages prove right the mobility of socially negotiated meanings of place, local culture and the dynamics of social boundaries in a global network: a space with the potential to blur such boundaries of difference and 'otherness'. As remarked on by Featherstone, postmodernist literature has a tendency to criticise fixed identity and celebrate disorder, but it has disregarded the fact that disorder has always been a varied part of life (1995:126-139). And never, if I may add, have cultural identities been more fixed than by the vivid dynamics of the social meanings that negotiate their values. Most importantly, as Jenkins pointed out to be a major overlooked theme of 'Barthian' ethnicity, is that groups are not distinct things as much as they are immanently changeable as products of ongoing interaction (1997:50). It is important to remember that there exists diversity amongst Inuit – a definition that covers different regional groups that again cover another set of different local groups. Within these many imagined communities, there are a number of ways for 'Inuit' to assert 'groupness'.

In regard to Kalaallit (Greenlanders) for instance, Dorais notes that the national identity is more important as a social frame of reference than an Inuit cultural identity, quite opposite to the case in Canada (1995/96). Ten years earlier, Petersen made a clear note on his own use of the word 'Greenlandic' to signify the same as 'Greenlandic Inuit' (1985:300). Hence, the negotiated meaning not only differs in social space but time as well. In a medium such as the Internet where Time-Space is compressed, the visibility of changes vividly exists, but this does not complicate things as much as it visualises the diversity and dynamics of Inuit identification.

The Arctic way of constructing Web pages breaks in on the transcendent myth of cyberspace, a myth where such boundary assertion is supposedly relegated to a secondary role because of the lack of physical matter in cyberspace – to quote Barlow in a moment of frustration: "Your legal concepts of property, expression, identity, movement, and context do not apply to us. They are based on matter, There is no matter here" (1996). While the lack of matter is certainly true in the strictest interpretation of its meaning, matter and local reality are nevertheless mirrored extensively, and not just on Inuit Web pages. Matter and locality are part of people's 'selves' and they can be used to localise, culturalise and personalise Web pages.

In text, some of the Web pages are constructed to describe the contemporary as well as the traditional life of Inuit in the Arctic; including the involvement of their local as well as regional diversity. Local histories, locales, localities, cultures, identities and environment are only some of the multiple choices for asserting dimensions wherein the local as well as cultural identity of Inuit is endowed. The contents of these Web pages are supplied by a broad range of schools, individuals, organisations, government, media, businesses, municipalities, artists, outfitters and travel agencies. For such reasons, the presence of local and cultural identity is identified on a large number of Web pages, but they differ, not only in regard to their purposes but also in regard to the diverse local reality that their producers are embedded in. Accordingly, the Web pages are products of a broad range of socially negotiated meanings within different communities – offline as well as online. This identification is closely linked with the relation to the 'other' of out-group members. The entries in guestbooks from different Web users from around the globe, as in the excerpts below, display the 'otherness' of 'us' and 'them' produced by the social interaction in and around these Web pages. The symbolic boundary markers in display are kinship, language, place, indigenousness and cultural artefacts:

The Chukchi Sea Trading Company, Guestbook, [Website] URL http://www.chukchi.com/. [visit: June 23, 2000]

"Seven years past I found out that I am ¼ Inupiat Eskimo on my mothers side. I am registered with the White Mountain/Fish River Village of White Mountain ..., (name removed by author)." Wa, USA – Sunday, November 29, 1998 at 22:41:50 (EST).

"Hello! I'm a postgraduate student at the Dept. of Saami Studies at Umeaa University in Sweden. I'm a Saami myself and been growing up in a boarding school. I'm planning to write my thesis about the Saami children who been living in boarding schools, and now I want to get in contact with other indigenous people who been growing up in boarding schools or residential school[s] ... Regards (name removed by author)." Sweden – Wednesday, February 11, 1998 at 05:01:48 (EST)

"I have very much enjoyed the visit to your home page. I especially like the ivory very much and would like to buy them too. Is buying ivory to Japan available too? Doomo Origato (thank you), (name removed by author)." Tokyo, Japan – Thursday, February 08, 1996 at 22:45:26 (PST)

It is evident that social boundaries are asserted on Web pages but, as boundaries, they are not similar to the ones that prevent people from entering a given space, as much as they display an identification of difference – which happens to be a difference that is also inviting for tourists and buyers of art. The boundaries are not fixed to certain issues: they are situationally applied by people and are found across different types of Web pages. Yet, the dynamics of this boundary assertion in guestbooks, images and text are not types of interaction as much as they represent the social organisation of people – emphasising 'me/us' and 'you/them', and referring to elements such as location, artefacts, kinship and language whereby they symbolically assert the difference. The constructed space of a Web page offers a platform for what is needed to negotiate 'self': difference or similarity between members of groups. Dybbroe finds in regard to self-determination amongst Inuit and Saami, that control of elements such as politics, culture, institutions, linguistics and education are focal for the expression of positive identity and avoidance of a stigmatised identity (1996:42). Web pages are similarly used to control this self-determined approach to identification. Note, in the excerpt of an online school essay, some of the major boundary markers of identification – ethnic identity, language and place:

> Leo Ussak Elementary School, Rankin Inlet, Nunavut, "Living in the North" by Nina Schweder. "We used to be called Eskimos, but now we are called Inuit, which means 'people' in our language, Inuktitut. People say that Rankin Inlet is going to get bigger in the future, but I think Rankin should stay the way it is because when it gets bigger, some kids might get lost. It is more fun when Rankin is small. I like living in Rankin Inlet. I've been here since I was born." [Web document] http://www.arctic.ca/LUS/Rankin_Inlet.html [visit: December 1, 1998].

Recursive dynamics:
social boundaries and cultural stuff

In the well-quoted "Ethnic groups and boundaries"(1969) ,Barth and others display specific interest in the processes where people assert ethnic identity by analysing the circumstances where groups/individuals change identity, or do not interact as usual (Barth 1994:174). They show specific interest in the social organisation of (ethnic) groups rather than the content of their cultures in an attempt to prevent the cultural stuff from becoming primordial characteristics of social groups – the cultural stuff being things such as material culture, tradition, language, religion, etc. The idea is that people continuously signify their cultures (cultural stuff) in different and new ways without loosing their identity as groups or the personal identity of belonging to a certain group: i.e. Inuit are still Inuit although they change their material culture and interact with other people. Hence, the social organisation must be what defines a group rather than its cultural traits. The paradigm of culture is regarded to be dynamic and mobile in the light of the social dynamics that negotiate its meaning.

In the Barthian sense, cultural traits do not define social organisation as much as social organisation defines what is understood by culture. Consequently, in a perspective of modernity and new information technology, this means that computers (material culture) in the lives of Inuit Web users do not characterise them as much as the ways they use this technology with relevance to their social organisation – i.e. the Inuit give the technology its meaning. In different studies on the identification of Inuit and Settlers in Labrador, the ways of doing things has been found to correlate with ethnic differences. For instance Richling finds that while Inuit prefer to shoot seals rather than catch them in nets such as the Settlers do, it is because they signify the different techniques on the basis of how they fit into their social organisation and economy (Richling 1989:71). Material culture such as speedboats, snowmobiles and rifles are not solely western objects. They are often adapted to certain ways of use that incorporate Inuit culture and social organisation. Somehow similar, Inuit Web pages are often constructed in ways that signify differences or similarities in regard to people and places, but their meanings, both as a product and a technology, are always changeable depending on the situation. In some cases they are culturally identified and in other cases they are just 'normal' Web pages. But often they are both, depending on the viewer's approach. The contents of their Web pages (sometimes cultural stuff) are chosen by the agents (Web masters) in regard to their expected value in social interaction[62]. Thus, although a number of Web pages are not constructed quite so overtly culturally, the presentation of certain symbols such as Inuksuits, flags or native language process a certain social meaning of interaction between social agents – Web masters and visitors.

Yet, according to the early thoughts of Barth[63], cultural traits are not focal to the assertion of ethnic identity as much as the dynamics of social boundaries (Barth 1969:15, Eriksen 1991: paragraph 8). Social boundaries are thought of as the relations that emerge and take place in and around the social agents (Inuit Web users), while the cultural stuff is cultural artefacts, clothing or symbols. Nevertheless, I have found that while I agree with Barth and others on the importance on social organisation, it is important to recognise the social use of cultural traits to assert difference – a point that has also been discussed by Jenkins (1997). On this account, I think of and identify social boundaries in relation to the importance by which people use the different symbols of physicality, place and culture for the assertion of difference, identity and locality. Thus, social boundaries can be expressed and processed on the Web with a minimum of direct social interaction between visitors and Web masters, but a maximum of delayed interaction though the imaging of symbols: text, maps, cultural artefacts, photographs and language. With the loss of dynamic face-to-face relationships, objects of identification become a major resource for the negotiated meaning of identification.

While photographic images of seal skin vests, mitts and slippers from a Web site such as *Arctic Creations*[64] in Iqaluit or the logo of the *Museum of Upernavik*[65] depicting a sketched drawing of a puppet from the abandoned settlement of Qattormiut all have valued cultural and symbolic significance, this is rather insignificant without social relations to signify the meaning of these objects. And it is also fair to say that an arts and crafts shop and a museum are not be likely to attract visitors without this cultural stuff. Hence, in many cases of 'cultural' Web sites, the importance of identifying difference is identified by a recursive relationship between social organisation and cultural content. In some cases the cultural dimension of something like the print *The Wind* by local Pangnirtung Print Shop artist Ida Karpik on *the Uqqurmiut Centre for Arts and Crafts* Web site[66] is not only an object for sale, but functions implicitly as a reason for social interaction between buyers and sellers in the first place. It invites the social negotiation of cultural identity and manifests Inuit culture in cyberspace. Similar means of identification are found on Web pages designed to attract and service tourists[67]. Constructing such a Web page or linking to it from another Web page, however, are only two out of many ways for a Web user to signify Web pages with social meaning and a sense of belonging. According to Cohen, almost any matter of perceived difference between in-group and out-group dimensions can be used to symbolise boundaries (1986:17).

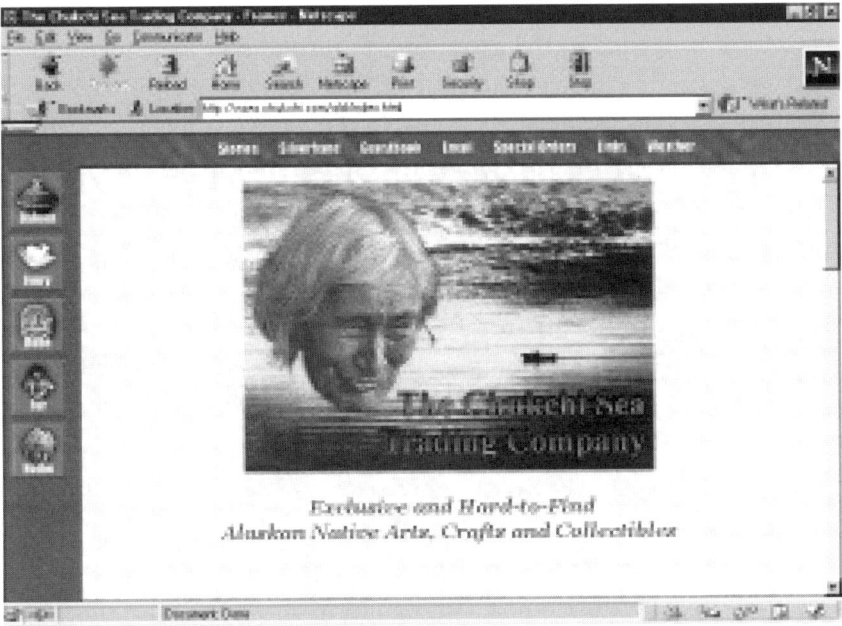

FIGURE 3 The Chukchi Sea Trading Company, an online as well as offline arts and crafts store, is located in Point Hope, Alaska. Note how the Web page displays culture, place, identity, physical space and peripherality [Web page] URL http://www.chukchi.com [visit: June 23, 2000].

Symbols or cultural traits of a great variety interact with social organisation, rather than being peripheral objects of social organisation. In an important contribution to the discussion of social boundaries and cultural stuff, Jenkins finds that religious differences in Northern Ireland, although they are not the source of conflict, nevertheless seem closely linked to the conflict. He concludes that: "boundaries, and the interaction across them, are intimately and indissolubly bound up with the cultural contents of ethnicity" (1997:120). Accordingly, cultural traits play a key role in identifying differences and similarities embedded in the social organisation of groups and the individuals associated with these. Along such lines, rather than seeing cultural traits and social organisation as two sorts of entities, I regard them to be different abstractions of daily life. Imagine the Chukchi Web page without images and cultural symbolism – it figures that social meaning, cultural stuff and physical images on Web pages often are propelled recursively.

By the same token, if I could remove those parts of text that refer to cultural traits on the following pages of the same Chukchi Web site, then identification would become more difficult to assert. Social organisation in regard to the assertion of cultural and local identity on the Web depends a great deal on the presence of cultural 'hints' or stuff to achieve meaning of identification – in text as well as images. Without this difference the social organisation looses much meaning on the Web page: the relation between browser and content is diffuse and meaning is replaced by feelings of semi-transcendence and deconstruction of cultural identity. Therefore, images and pieces of text that refer to cultural traits are immensely important on Web sites such as the Chukchi Sea Trading Company of Point Hope, as they swiftly assert 'otherness' or sense of belonging or not for the visitors. This is what their customers come looking for and this is what the Web master serves – a socially negotiated meaning of identification that is recognised by in-group as well as out-group visitors.

It becomes increasingly clear that the stress on the importance of social organisation needs the support of a theory on symbolic identification: One such theory in general is delivered by Cohen (1985, 1986) who studies the meanings that symbols have for the idea of belonging to a community. Thus, where Barth argues the need for analysis of the social *form* instead of the cultural *content*, Cohen advocates the need to focus on *meaning* of culture rather than form and structure (Cohen 1985:71). While it could seem that the two scholars disagree, they actually supplement each other, as they are both interested in investigating the process of social organisation. Jenkins (1997) picks up on Cohen's stress on meaning of content, and all three authorities acknowledge that the dynamic meaning of community/social organisation is asserted through shifting meanings that are socially processed amongst in-group as well as out-group.

Us and them: self-identify by identifying others

In Mitra's article on Web pages with an affiliation to India or Indians (1997), he argues that there are several ways in which an audience can make use of and understand Web pages. He uncovers some of the dynamics of out-group and in-group discourse affecting how people read, view and understand the content of a Web page and of how they read hypertext.

If one imagines a single Web page as one page in a huge text by the name of the World Wide Web, then clicking on a link, whether it is a link to a page at the same Web site or a link to a page at another site, takes one to another Web page in the hypertext. The hypertext is the text that the user establishes by clicking around the different pages. All depending on the similarity between pages, the effect can be one of "seamlessness". However, the experience can also be the opposite where the browsing person does not understand the content: for example because of language, religion or other cultural aspects.

Some of the musical or religious pages referred to in Mitra's study demand in-depth knowledge from the audience for specific parts of Indian language, culture and society: such as knowing who Shahrukh Khan is, what karNAtaka music is or what the Hindu scriptures, *Bhagavad-Geeta*, entail. The correlation between the pages and their choice of language and symbols like flags, maps, pictures of Indian movie-stars or religious icons create coherence or chaos depending on who the audience is and what hypertext they choose or are suggested to view. A person surfing the Web casually or searching for specific material creates his or her own hypertext, depending on the Web pages chosen. Naturally, the opportunities and choices are also influenced by what the Web masters make available, the content they publish or the links to Web pages that they choose to make available. These hyper-links assert strategic meanings of the page, if you will, they substantiate and make the page more interesting for their audience. Hence, as argued on a previous occasion, a Web page can be constructed to promote itself by promoting others. By referring to social relations through a number of links to other Web pages that connote a certain social organisation (boundaries) of people, such as Arviat in Nunavut, in the case of Eric Anoee's Web page, or by asserting the social boundary in text, the Web page mirrors social meaning on different levels – meanings with a socio-physical relevance to assertion place and identity in process of identification between out-group and in-group members. See for instance the two excerpts from the Web pages of two businesses from Clyde River and Pangnirtung (both in Nunavut) introducing themselves by belonging to a certain place: a distinction that helps to add authenticity to themselves as well as the products and services they sell:

> "Clyde River is located 70° 28′ N 68° 36′ W on Baffin Island, Canada. An Inuit community of 600+ residents, Clyde River is becoming one of the fastest growing new tourist destinations on Baffin Island." (Levi Palituq Outfitting 1998). [Web document] URL http://www. nuna net.com/~palituq/main1.html [visit: December 12, 1998].

> "Pangnirtung Fisheries is a modern fish processing plant located in the picturesque Inuit community of Pangnirtung in a fjord of Cumberland Sound on Baffin Island." [Web document] URL http://www.arctic-can.nt.ca/pang fish/in-dex.html [visit: December 12, 1998].

The assertion of cultural/local identity on the Web as elsewhere is focal for the process of distinction: i.e. 'you' are there and 'we' are here. Distance and peripherality are used as a resource to generate this sort of social meaning. In regard to the dynamics of hypertext (the text that every Web page is a part of) Erickson finds that: "Something curious is happening on the World Wide Web. It is undergoing a slow transformation from an abstract, chaotic, information Web into what I call a social hypertext" (1996: paragraph 1). It is equally important to recognise that hypertext is socially negotiated not only because of its networked meaning on the Web but also because of the mirrored meaning that users invoke from outside cyberspace. Thus, the hypertext refers to an existing system of socially negotiated meaning in a new dimension. It is this social hypertext that I am partly focused on, across categories of many types or genres of Web pages, and across notions that separate cyberspace and physical space. The approach explores symbolic boundaries that help to assert a differentiating discourse between in-group and out-group. On the subject of the examples provided, one should be aware that Web pages are seldom permanent but are rather a dynamic inference of change of content over time, making it impossible to know what will change or when it will (Walters 1996: paragraph 3, section 4.1). The dynamics of text and images are recursive mirrors of the general dynamics of identity and place as platforms of social meaning.

Taloyoak in cyberspace

The main example of this chapter is the Taloyoak community Web site[68]. The Web pages within the site are comprehensive in their constructed meanings to assert local and cultural identity in cyberspace. It is not a typical Web site, if there is such a thing, but a site that exemplifies a set of different ways to negotiate meanings of identification on the Web. While it cannot represent all other Web sites to be found, it serves as an example for some of the methods open to the assertion of social boundaries: local as well as cultural identities.

The boundaries of social meaning are, to repeat the argument of Cohen, able to let almost any matter of perceived difference between in-group and out-group symbolise their boundaries (1986:17). Similarly, the Taloyoak Web site includes a wide range of information: it has lists on members of local associations; a section on local history; a map of Nunavut; different prices on sea and air-borne food in the local store; texts and symbols about language and cultural identity; as well as a business directory with photographs of the offices and links to other Web pages from the community as well as Nunavut. Thus the Web pages identify several dimensions of belonging: place, region, community, associations, culture, language, Arctic cost of living, a shared history and photographs of houses. All together, the information and content of this page questions the utopian idea of transcendent non-space, where elements such as ethnic identity and geography supposedly have no claims or do not exist, as these are apparently based on matter.

The Information page[69] of the Web site reveals a local history, from which I have summarised some of the content. Taloyoak is a community of 648 people, constituting the Northernmost community on the Canadian mainland in Nunavut. Taloyoak is Inuktitut for "large caribou blind", and refers to the stone caribou blind traditionally used by the Inuit, who are locally known as the Netsilik Inuit or Netsilingmiut[70], to corral and harvest caribou. Their descendants presently make up some 92 per cent of the population in the community that was formed after 1948 when the Hudson Bay Company relocated to this spot from further north because of poor ice conditions. Since then, the community grew as the Catholic and Anglican missionaries, the Royal Canadian Mounted Police and Inuit resettled or were relocated here. The community still has hunting and trapping as a vital part of everyday life, as well as a thriving arts and crafts production.

The community Web pages are maintained by a Web master from the Taloyoak Broadcasting Society, which consists of some 160 individuals. In co-operation with the "Community Access Programme"[71] (CAP) funded by Industry Canada to set up access centres in rural communities and the "Community Initiatives Program" set up by the Government of the Northwest Territories, the society is obliged to maintain a community profile on the Internet. Some of the objectives of these pages are to provide people with ideas of what it is like to live in Taloyoak, which among other things is hoped to improve tourism and business opportunities for the community. Other CAP sites are found in Rankin Inlet[72] and Arviat[73].

Two access centres in Taloyoak have been established: one at the local Netsilik School and the other at the Taloyoak Training Centre. The two centres complement each other in opening hours as well as in equipment: Macintosh, PCs, scanners, digital cameras, Quickcams and a wide range of software, and among other things Web publishing software. The pages are hoped to inspire others in the community to make use of the Internet, according to Bohlender, the Secretary Treasurer (personal communication, 1998). The advantages hoped to be gained

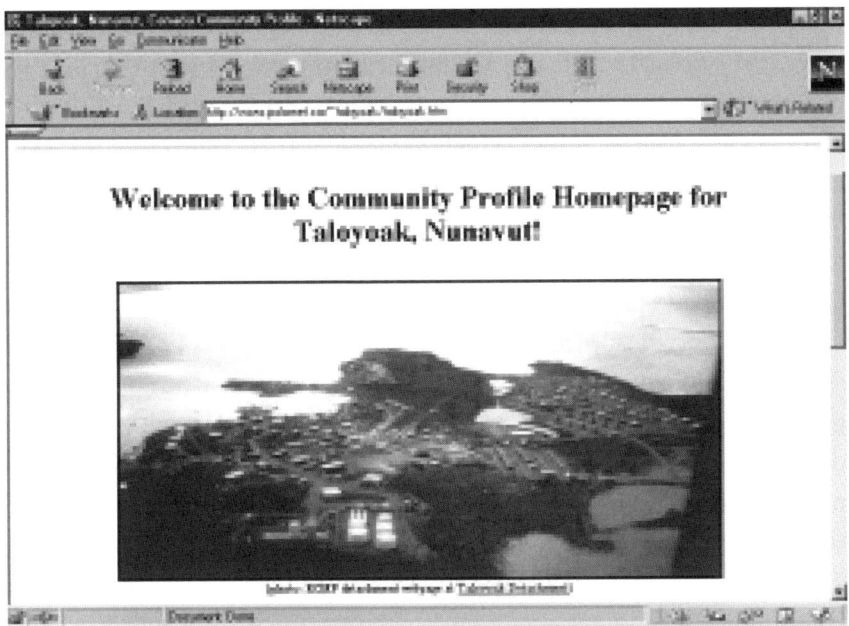

FIGURE 4 The Taloyoak Community Profile Web pages. Such photographs are not uncommon and help to mirror physicality on the Net [Web page] URL http://www.polarnet.ca/~taloyoak/taloyoak.htm [visit: June 23, 2000].FIGURE 4 The Taloyoak Community Profile Web pages. Such photographs are not uncommon and help to mirror physicality on the Net [Web page] URL http://www.polarnet.ca/~taloyoak/taloyoak.htm [visit: June 23, 2000].

through the process are economic, social and cultural, and are implemented through different partnerships between national, provincial territorial, regional and local bodies.

The Web site is split into two halves: one for the local Netsilik school[74] and one for the Taloyoak Training Centre. Both halves function as access centres for the public. When viewing the Web page of the Taloyoak community profile Web page[75] – part of the training centre's Web site – one is first met by the text "Welcome to the Community Profile Homepage for Taloyoak, Nunavut!" together with an aerial photograph of the community supplied by the local Royal Canadian Mounted Police detachment in Taloyoak. Below, at the time of research, one finds a short introductory note about the Taloyoak Broadcasting Society (TBS) that maintains the Web site and seven links to the categories Information, Recreation, Attractions, Accommodations, Business, Services, TBS and an extra link to the Canadian Access Programme (CAP). As mentioned before information of the site describes the community for the browsing person. Among the available resources, one can find links to the NWT Bureau of Statistics, the local Internet service provider (ISP) Polarnet[76], Taluq Design Ltd[77] that make traditional dolls and puppets, First Air[78] that services the community and the Nunavut Handbook (a tourist guide), which has a section on Taloyoak[79]. In addition, the Web site contains an e-mail directory[80] (17 addresses), a 'Who's Who' directory[81] as well as a Hamlet Phone directory.

Other Web pages negotiate the meaning of local identity as well: quite a few Greenlandic municipalities have maintained their own Web sites since 1997. The contents of their Web sites centre around the same themes as that of Taloyoak, but are more focused on the administrative dimensions of the communities. Still, themes such as tourism, businesses, brief local histories, links to local Web pages and pictures from the local area are commonly used in the construction of these pages. The Nuuk municipality[82] in Greenland has a comprehensive Web site containing local documents from the city council meetings as well as legislative documents from the Greenlandic government. In Qaanaaq, Greenland, one can similarly find a Web site constructed by the municipal Department of Culture[83] (Kultur og Undervisningsforvaltningen) with an emphasis on local history, pictures and tourism. In Alaska the representation of communities is mostly taken care of by schools such as the Nuiqisut Trapper School[84], with basic information about the village of Nuiqisut, or the Harold Kaveolok School[85] in Kaktovik, on Barter Island. A Web site such as the Canadian Pan Arctic Inuit Logistics Corporation[86] Web site functions both as the public face of the corporation as well as a resource for Web pages of the Canadian Inuit community. The Ilulissat Trade Council[87] in Greenland maintains a site with information on local businesses, accommodation and other local services in the same fashion as the Web pages of the Kodiak Chamber of Commerce[88].

Consequently, the dimension of the community depends on the purposes of the Web sites – varying from the Taloyoak pages, the home pages of Eric Anoee or KalaK's Greenland, to the Inuit Circumpolar Conference (ICC)[89] Web pages. It is fair to say that such community and identity affirming Web pages generally represent a socialising offline community and a symbolic or representative online community. According to Bohlender, the Web master of the Taloyoak Web site, the idea is to provide people with some idea of what it is like to live in their part of the world: the linking of Web pages to the site helps visitors to get a more complete image of the community.

When searching for Taloyoak through the popular search engine Altavista, the search comes up with 360 Web pages[90], which, compared to the 648 people actually living there, is a substantial number of Web pages. However, most of these Web pages are not created by the inhabitants of the community, but by others, and their contents range from single word mentions of Taloyoak to entire pages being about nothing else but the community. Still, the relational dimension of social or symbolic boundaries is apparent in these processes of identity affirmation. Web pages not even made by Inuit thereby still help to reflect some sort of Inuit identity – potentially adding to the Taloyoak hypertext.

Web pages, such as the third reference from the search "Taloyoak (Spence Bay) page" from the Arctic Perspectives Web site, situates the community with a physical map – north of Gjoa Haven, east of Cambridge Bay and north-west of Pelly Bay. At the top of the page there is a series of links to other communities and themes about the Arctic. The more specific Taloyoak information is split into a short story about the deceased Inuit ivory carver Karoo Ashevak, information about the importance of hunting for the local Inuit and lastly a section on traditional knowledge and the importance of elders in the community. Although the content is specifically about the community, it is basic to understand and mostly meant for people outside the community, as the understanding and knowledge of any community member would go far beyond that indicated by such information. There is no hyperlink from this page to the previously described "Taloyoak community profile page" but instead one is led to a statistical profile on the community, as supplied by the NWT Bureau of Statistics. A little outdated (from 1995), it gives the visitor an idea about income, gender, language, age and, for example, a cost of living index number that is 195 compared to Edmonton's 100. Other Web pages retrieved from the search are mostly simple documents where the name Taloyoak appears without much explanation.

Following such a procedure, one should indeed consider that there are several ways of reading Taloyoak hypertext on the Web, some being related to tourism and travel guides, others to organisations, businesses, individuals, reports and other online documents. The process of asserting Taloyoak in cyberspace as an Inuit village is dynamic and not controlled from one place. All depending on the hypertext chosen, the experience is different but still one that identifies a rural/peripheral Arctic community associated with Inuit identity and culture.

Mitra notes that the segmentation of content responds to the audience of diasporic Indians around the world: i.e. people who live apart but who share some degree of commonality (1997:162). In the case of the Taloyoak community pages, these rather address a segmented audience who do not know about the community – the community does not exist online as much as it does offline. Naturally, the online presence will catch the attention of local visitors who are already familiar the community, but the purpose is educative and informative, essentially for reaching those who do not know about the community. Meanwhile, the locals still continue to socialise as a community in physical space.

During research, a printed screen-shot of the Taloyoak Web page was lying about in a computer room at the University of Aberdeen where it was consequently noticed by several students at different occasions. The page displayed a large aerial photo of the Arctic community and was, in regard to the research, thought to illustrate the embedding of physical space and place in cyberspace. The reactions – discussed below – remind us that identification is a negotiation between how some choose to inform about themselves and how others choose to try to understand.

The general but still different reactions among the students who had little or no experience with the Arctic was to focus on the oil-tanks or the symmetric roads and, as a result, regarded the picture as having little to do with their own conceptions of what an Arctic community would or should look like. They imagined an Arctic community to have snow, no roads and definitely no oil-tanks: some even asked, without a hint of humour, why there were no igloos present. Their focus was on basic things in the community, prompting them to draw rather large conclusions. Although these people made their judgements on physical dimensions more than social dimensions, they interpreted the Web page very differently from the people at the University who had some experience with the Arctic. For this second group, the picture looked nothing less than a rather ordinary Arctic community.

What seemingly was just an aerial shot of an Arctic community for some, was for others the epitome of industrialisation, loss of culture, Westernisation, cultural imperialism and more, within that discourse. That it was all a product mediated by the Internet collided even more with a romantic illusions of the Arctic, as if technology itself presented a contradiction to Inuit cultures.

Indeed, the deceptive dichotomy between indigenous peoples and modern technology is very much alive: not surprisingly, chiefly among others than the indigenous peoples themselves. One is regrettably forced to suggest, that some students' romantic impressions about the Arctic and the Inuit are both sad and comic at the same time. In similar vein, Mitra presents the dilemma that arises when pages have to address both a small community as well as a global audience, "... thus placing greater interpretative demand on the text" (1997:160). The meaning of identification is a constant negotiation between self-identification and being identified by others.

Large proportions of Web pages that reaffirm Inuit identity are intended for global as well as local audiences. That their messages can clash with other people's conceptions illuminates not only the relational aspect of identity formation but also the educative potential in the existence of local/cultural Web pages. From a humorous perspective, the Qitsualik Web site[91] has a section with frequently asked questions, one of which is "How do Inuit have sex?" The answer of course is "Privately!" The two excerpts below denote these educational perspectives:

> "It is my hope that information about Inuit and all aspects of our culture will bring more understanding and interest for the Inuit people, and our sustainable ways of life." Male, Nuuk, (personal communication, 1998).

> "I think the use of the Internet expands knowledge of Inuit culture, as well as represents Alaska and the Arctic as an

international visitor destination." Female, Barrow, Alaska (personal communication, 1998).

Within such realms, Web pages have an effect on the potential ignorance. Looking through the sites, one comes across large amounts of material that identifies different aspects of local life for the people outside the group, sometimes explaining in foreign languages the elements that are already well-known to the local in-group. The Internet delivers opportunities for Inuit to bring their own messages across, avoiding the denotations of Arctic nature movies – beautiful as they may be – the polemic of extreme environmentalist organisations, the general disinterest of mass media and the potential irradiate political discourse undertaken far away from the immediacy of Inuit. As some argue, the world outside the Arctic tends to forget that people actually live there, often focusing more on nature – unless the inhabitants can be shown in what is believed to be a harmonic context with nature by Western standards. What was simply a photograph on a Web page challenged the assumptions of some Scottish university students: a computer-mediated challenge that consequently has or is hoped to have educational potential for Inuit and their relationships with other people. The particular use of the Web to reflect upon and inform about life in the Arctic is a recognised potential usually linked to the worldwide, legitimate assertion of local and cultural identity. The examples are numerous and Inuit know all too well that they themselves might be holding the key to self-determination, but other people's perceptions represent the keyhole, if you will.

Native Language on the Web

The amount of socio-cultural content on Inuit Web pages which is so specific and particular that it addresses solely Inuit is limited. Sometimes it even seems as if the more culture-specific sites like the Canadian *Qitsualik, Arctic & Inuit* by Rachel Qitsualik, are frequented mostly by non-Inuit – judging by the entries of the discussion forum and the F.A.Q. page about Inuit and the Arctic. Mitra notes that these are likely the popular pages which have to address both in-group and out-group (1997:164). In regard to Inuktitut, the language spoken by Canadian eastern Arctic Inuit, Dorais has found in the Québec community of Puijilik that Inuktitut is mostly sufficient at local level, but the language is replaced by English or French when communication reaches beyond the village limits – even within the Inuit organisations. Inuktitut as a language is linked to basic identity and means of expression for the local, and it is recognised at a national level as a cultural signifier and ideological object (1991). This suggests that the lack of Inuktitut on the Web should not be taken as a sudden lack but as a feature of language and communication that is related to offline as well as online practicality.

Language as a cultural significant is not necessarily a way of keeping others out, as Mitra argues: in many cases it is quite the opposite. While it is provides a sanction against outside members on some Web pages, it also works as a cultural signifier that attracts audiences, on others. However, rather than being strategically used as an excluding tool on Web pages, Inuktitut is used as a service to Inuktitut speaking Inuit. If visitors are looking to find Inuit culture on the Web, language, even though it is incomprehensible, is bound to be one of those elements that will attract them.

The most common and easiest way to achieve the explicit distinction between out-group and in-group members is by using distinctive language. Such an example is the Greenlandic left-wing political party, Inuit Ataqatigiit, who maintain a Web site entirely in Greenlandic, apart from the parliamentary transcriptions that are in Danish. In the guestbooks of the political parties Siumut and Inuit Ataqatigiit, the majority of entries are written in Greenlandic. Naturally, as these political pages address local rather than a worldwide audience, the language used is often entirely Greenlandic. And there are several reasons for this discrepancy between the many Web pages in Danish compared to the overly political discussion in Greenlandic. The presence of Greenlandic language on the Web differs according to the skill and resources of the Web master as well as to the purpose of the Web site. Some municipal Web sites such as the afore mentioned Nuuk Municipality is tri-lingual in Greenlandic, Danish and English, yet with far less content in English than in the two other languages. It is normal to experience the use of Greenlandic language in chat for a, such as Piteraq[92], or in the guestbooks of various Web sites.

FIGURE 5 The Inuit Ataqatigiit, a political party in Greenland, has one of the few examples of a Greenlandic Web site with the majority of its content in Greenlandic, rather than Danish or English [Web page] URL http://www.ia.gl [visit: June 23, 2000].

As argued earlier, many Web pages address people who are not local. But, as pointed out by a Web user during fieldwork, the local population perhaps does not want Danes to interfere in their political discussions. And certainly this is not a question of ability since those currently producing pages are often educated people, fluent in Danish and/or English. Indeed, these guestbooks are good examples of an out-group/in-group discourse or an example of what Barth and others refer to as boundary maintenance. The Greenlandic language with its estimated 49,850 speakers[93], which includes Greenlanders living abroad (Fortescue 1998:8), has the potential to limit the understanding and accessibility for millions of other users. However, the use of Greenlandic to address a local audience has yet to be generally employed on behalf of the Web masters and quite a few Greenlandic pages already are, or are planning to become, bi or tri-lingual – Greenlandic, Danish and/or English. Clearly such an approach indicates an expected audience extending beyond the physical and social boundaries of the Greenlandic speaking population and is an example of supplying some amount of in-group information for a worldwide audience. On a practical level, however, it is most commonly done by supplying lesser amounts of information in foreign language than in the main-language of the Web site. With a steady increase of Web pages during the last couple of years, the amount of Web content in Greenlandic is growing – especially on personal Web pages.

In Canada the development and implementation of Inuktitut Syllabic characters in computers could produce a growing amount of pages in native language, as it is has been documented that more communication in native language is of interest to many Canadian Inuit (Canadian Broadcasting Company 1994, Christensen 1998, Thomas 1998). But so far, only a few Web sites have taken on the implementation and production of content in Inuktitut or Inuttitut syllabics: Nunavut.com[94], Nunatsiaq News[95], Avataq Cultural Institute[96] and Inuit Uqausingita Taiguusingit/Arviat District Education Authority[97] (the district authority maintains a Web site with an Inuktitut Pictionary). Other Web pages have a symbolic use of syllabics in images, logos and headings, such as the Web pages of the Qikitaaluk Corporation[98], the Qikiqtani Inuit Association[99] or the Makivik Corporation[100]. It is noticeable that none of these Web pages are personal. The reason is twofold: firstly, individuals seem to construct Web pages mostly for the larger audience, i.e. an audience that exceeds the Canadian Arctic; secondly, the construction of bilingual Web sites demands time as well as skill.

On Alaskan Web pages, one hardly finds any pages in Yup'ik or Iñupiat languages, apart from the occasional word or sentence. Generally, for all three regions, the chances of finding native language rather than English, Danish or French is most likely to occur when reading contributions from the audience in the guestbooks. Hence, relations and statements that in the end help to reaffirm social boundaries for both in-group and out-group members are not purely dictated or authored by the Web masters but by the users of their pages.

Guestbooks

Depending on the situation, social boundaries can be truly situational, adaptive, excluding, un-restrictive and restrictive: deployed using diverse incentives and strategies, offering different results. And although maintaining boundaries comes naturally to everybody in practice, allowing one to identify others as well as to identify oneself, these pre-set rules of conduct are necessarily a worded abstraction when explained. It is also important to stress that, compared to offline space, the circumstances for online space might differ, but that the sort of boundary maintenance found on the Web neither differs from what is 'normal' nor is it necessarily more complex.

Below are some samples from entries in the guestbook at the *Labrador Inuit Association's* Web site. The chosen entries have been written by visitors from Iran, Greenland, Canada and USA. They provide us with a glimpse of the boundaries that emerge and confirm, through the use of guestbooks and bulletin boards, how little it takes to dispatch signals affirming separate group identities:

> Labrador Inuit Association, Guestbook [Web site] URL http://www.cancom.net/~franklia/main.html[visit: December 10, 1998].

> Record 161. Name: (removed by author). Referred by: Net Search. From: Greenland. Date/time: 1998-12-09 02:29:00. Comments: "Ajunngissusia Kiisami nassaaraassi ujartaraluarlusi Uanga Nuummiuuvunga naak Qaqortumiit nuunnerullunga qavani Kalaallit Nunatta kujataanit. Arlassi soqutiginnissaguni allaffigiinnarsinnaavaannga kalaallisut imaluunniit tuluttut. Ajunngikkisi takuss. Own translation: "Good – I finally found you, although by coincidence – even though I was looking for you. I'm from Nuuk, although I've actually moved here from Qaqortoq in Southern Greenland. If somebody should be interested at some point, he or she is welcome to write me in either Greenlandic or English. Take care."

Record 140. Name: (removed by author). Referred by: Net Search. From: Happy Valley, Labrador. Date/time: 1998-10-13 16:06:00. Comments: "It was very inspiring for me to visit the Labrador Inuit Homepage. Actually it made me a little homesick. I am an Inuk who was born and raised in Happy Valley. I understand how difficult and sometimes frustrating it can be to prepare for an environmental review assessment ...[I]n friendship, (name removed by author)."

Record 117. Name: (removed by author). Referred by: From a Friend. From: Iran. Date/time: 1998-07-23 10:57:00. Comments: "I am interested in your activities. I have no comment yet. Will write more later."

Record 113. Name: (removed by author). Referred by: Word of Mouth. From: Hopedale, now in Texas. Date/time: 1998-07-12 21:07:00. Comments: "ILLETANAMEK ILLUNASE I am living in FORT WORTH now just thought I would say hello to all my family the ABLES, ROLAND & PATRICIA KEMUKSIGAK, BUDDY JACQUE, and the FLOWERS. I love and miss you all very much. Take very good care of yourselves, (names removed by author) of FORT WORTH, TEXAS."

These are responses that recognise the given affiliation of the Web pages to the identification of Labrador Inuit – covering such recognition within themes of local, regional, national and international dimensions. The reactions to the Arctic space reflected in the Web site are expressed geographically, socially, culturally and by language – all being aspects wherein social boundaries exist. Not only do the respondents address Inuit as a social group, some affirm themselves as Inuit through this recognition, while others show that they are not part of this group or its physical location, but have an interest. Hence, one of the above reactions is in Greenlandic, which is close to the Inuit dialect spoken in Labrador, affirming both Greenlandic identity and commonality with Labrador Inuit, and demonstrating general Inuit identity for the excluded onlooker without proficiency in the language. A second person writes that he is from Iran, while a third makes it explicit that, although she is now living in Texas, she is originally from Hopedale (Labrador) and uses Inuktitut as well as social relations to highlight her case.

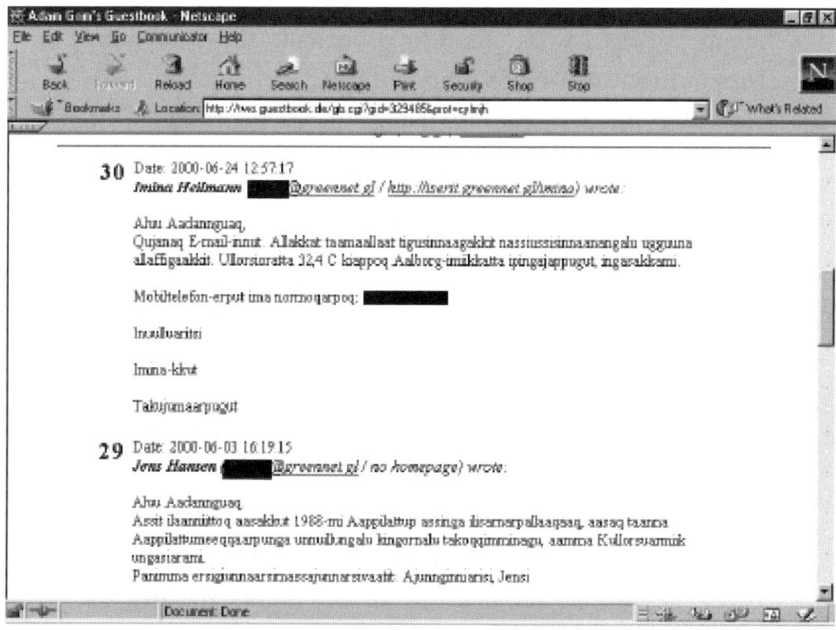

FIGURE 6 From the guestbook of the Grim family. The entries are often made by friends in Greenland or, as shown, by a friend on a trip to Denmark during a heat wave [Web page] URL http://iserit.greennet.gl/adamgrim/ [visit: June 24, 2000].

Identification relates to specifications in topics such as kinship, heritage, friends, location of birth and location of residence. In regard to the Internet, references to kinship are not always applicable since users communicate far beyond the normal outreach of family extensions, although, in some cases, when people address specific people in communities, as the woman from Hopedale does in the example above, this assertion is made with reference to kinship and friends[101]. Instead the family denominator is turned into ethnic identity – i.e. being Inuit or not – or other social spheres relating to a specific community.

It is beyond question that pages on the World Wide Web contain many spatial references to the residential locations of users in physical space – through images and symbols on Web pages, references in text produced by Web masters and text produced by browsing people. Accordingly, it seems that identity and physicality play integral roles in asserting social boundaries, belonging and commonality, not only in guestbooks, but on ordinary Web pages as well.

The deficiency in face-to-face response from a guestbook does not prevent one from seeking a sense of belonging, commonality or difference within the realm of the space being visited. When an Inuk makes an entry into a guestbook, belonging to a page affiliated with Inuit identity, a reference to commonality is often made by writing in native tongue, referring to specific people, locations and events. This can be seen on Web pages like the Inuvik home Page, Family Grim's home page, Qitsualik Web site, Chuckci Sea Trading Company and other pages with guestbooks. Most of all, the entries try to establish a social relation, not one that necessarily develops into further communication between Web masters and visitors, but one that affirms, at least on screen, a social relation – acknowledged whether or not the visitor is an offline in-group member for the visited space.

In a development to this idea, an informant to Chandler finds that predicaments arise when people feel too familiar with the Web master, yet completely disregarding that this familiarity is not reciprocal (Chandler 1998, paragraph 7, section 6). Indeed, the rather easy-going atmosphere on the Internet, partially driven by levels of anonymity and non-physical contact, make the first step in contact easy. Some entries of out-group members will often try to assert some kind of commonality with their hosts, by writing entries that either flatter or confirm some knowledge about Inuit and the Arctic. The statements vary in length from punchlines to small essays about personal history or a political or cultural issue relevant to the Web page visited.

Intelligible boundaries

The use of the Web helps to assert, identify and negotiate the meaning of Inuit identity, or rather identities. While there is an ongoing pan-Arctic assertion of Inuit identity on the Web, as in the case of the ICC Web site, cultural identity on the Web is currently linked mostly with the identification of local identities rather than a single Inuit identity. While the evidence of local diversity has suffered somewhat from my approach to Web page analysis, I have limited my discussion to a modest number of different Web sites. The few selected examples will serve, if not as a representative example of the cultural/local diversity of Inuit, then as a good example of how identity can be manifested and negotiated in cyberspace.

Generally speaking, in the case of Alaska, cultural identification often takes place on the Web pages of native corporations or businesses, while the symbolic use of text, images and cultural artefacts is similar to that of Canadian cases. Greenlandic Web pages seem to differ in the way in which they identify a national and local identity rather than an ethnic one. The processes of identification are dynamic and relational in time and space, resting not only upon Inuit, but on other users as well. A commonly recognised potential of the Internet, amongst Inuit users that I communicated with, is that it enables them to incorporate aspects of group identity into their relations with other people – something previous mass media left less option for, as the Inuit controlled media was limited to the local region or area.

The Web pages discussed in this chapter prove a specific consciousness amongst some Inuit: commercial, organisational and individually, or else a will to represent themselves as Inuit with non-erasable bonds to offline space and sociality; a measurement making them no less "real" Internet users than Inuit – they are both. Through the sort of identity affirming use discussed here, Inuit and others are partly following the general notion of the Internet to make it as real as possible (virtual reality). However, they are not necessarily pursuing this trend within the possibilities of creating cyber-identities dependent on the Internet for their existence. They, or at least some of them, are affirming and reproducing their offline identities online. As such, the Internet, as a technology or a trend within globalisation, plays a double-role: while more than likely being a medium of bringing other people's reality closer to distant rural communities, be they good or bad, it is also a way of bringing reflections of Inuit reality closer to distant parts of the same world. This process has been recognised by Jenkins, who states that: "Localism and ethnicity are conceptualised as two sides of the same coin and each may (re)assert itself either as a defensive reaction to, or a result of, the increasingly global context of social life" (1997:43).

In my survey, a majority of 71 per cent of the users believed the Internet to promote an equal exchange between the Arctic and the rest of the world. Generally they did not consider the Internet to produce an overflow of information and foreign culture into Inuit society, but they were aware of the potential risk. Clearly Inuit seem to have few, if any, problems advocating local, ethnic and cultural issues in cyberspace. Thus, the encroachment upon Inuit identity by others, potentially fuelled further by the increasing use of the globalising Internet, also seems to be simultaneously lifting the recognised importance in asserting Inuit identity by handling the medium in ways specific to Inuit identity and needs. In many concerns this sort of globalisation seems to be about localisation, providing local content for a worldwide population[102]. As noted earlier, reports such as *Connecting the North: Defining Users' Needs* (IBC 1994) and the national IT strategy for Greenland (IT-Råd [The IT Council for Greenland] 2000) prove a general interest amongst users and non-users to utilise the medium in particular culture specific ways supposed to promote local and regional aspects of culture, economy, health and education. In this way, rather than seeing the presence of other people on the Internet as a cultural threat, their presence is regarded as the very potential of the network. What becomes the medium of encroachment, simultaneously becomes the medium for a reaction against the same. It is probably not a question of avoiding the Internet, but of instead mastering its use in self-determined ways from as early as possible:

> "It's the Western ways that we have to meet and live with, so why not promote ourselves any possible way we can and make more money at it to live better than we have in the past." Male, Alaska (personal communication 1998).

A large number of pages address local, regional and national identity in as many ways one can imagine: from local advertising about TV Bingo on the Inuvik home page, Canada, from the Web page for a Grill Bar in Qaqortoq[103], Greenland, from the Nunamiut School of Anaktuvuk Pass[104], Alaska, to organisations like the Kitikmeot Inuit Association[105], or to corporations such as the Makivik Corporation[106] and to governments such as the Greenland Home Rule Government[107], or a series of

Nunavut governmental bodies and the Web pages of the ICC[108]. Their pages negotiate different meanings of identity and community. The Internet does not mythically and automatically dissolve boundaries that are so very important for the daily value of people's lives. Naturally, Web users are prone to be affected by other people's values and ideas on the Internet. Their outwards orientation, also shown in the linking of Web pages to international software and hardware companies, foreign radio stations, online newspapers and online friends of individuals living on the others side of the globe, does not necessarily make them any less local. Thus, the social relations that emerge from Internet use can just as well evolve around cultural and local particularism.

> "There are three individuals from Ireland, Sweden and Belgium whom I communicate regularly with, all relating to my Inuit heritage, whether it be about usage of Inuktitut language or cultural traditions. I have also learned about these individuals' cultures too, though I have known about them before, but more in-depth now." Male, Iqaluit, Nunavut (personal communication 1998).

Just as the Internet can be used to break down social boundaries, it can just as well be used to assert or maintain the same or other boundaries. There is little argument to deterministically regard Inuit less Inuit by their use of this medium, nor propose that it will make them more Inuit in the future. As discussed in other cases, Inuit have continued to consider themselves as Inuit, within the diversity of the distinction, despite their integration of Western culture and technology[109]. In this regard, the so-called *non-space* opportunities of cyberspace celebrated by utopians and feared by dystopians, do not seriously question the reality of boundary-affirming Web pages. They often seem to be dealing with abstract "global-babble" that is superficially driven on a "high level of generality" (Hannerz 1992:34) compared to the more practical aspects of Internet usage: there are many ways of using the Internet that go between the extremes of polarised scenarios. Whether Inuit boundaries lie within several dimensions of life, such as rurality, sociality, territoriality, ethnicity or others, they all provide cyberspace with an already known substance. They make the Web rather intelligible by reflecting upon common categories of interaction that are accepted by themselves and other people.

As my discussion has hopefully shown, the identification of social boundaries on the Web is processed through many likely and, one it tempted to say, unlikely channels: the social references found in guestbooks, information about Inuit communities, cultural artefacts vended through online galleries and the use of native language or symbols. Important in regard to these processes of socio-symbolic boundary production and identity affirmation is that it is not to say beforehand how or when a visitor stumbles over, or starts looking for, these Web pages, how the person reacts to them, or how and for how long these identity affirming relations exist. However, it is safe to say that the likely outcome is an affirmation and recognition of Inuit identity – an identity relating to both sociality and territoriality, as well as offline and online space.

Last but not least, my discussions have revolved around general Inuit culture and identity through a rather culture-specific use of the Web and as such they cover only a minimal part of the Internet use. Furthermore, they do this on a generalising basis. This picture of specific cultural and identity asserting use has naturally been extrapolated by the focus, but nevertheless, within such use, I find a strong local and cultural presence of Inuit Web pages closely connected to a wide array of commercial, organisational and personal interests. A static view of the dynamics of technology, culture and identity would support such an ideological assumption that these dynamics of identity cannot bridge the 'gap' between offline and online space, or that indigenous culture is inconsistent with modern technology. An issue discussed by Sejersen concerns the conflict between Inuit and the International Whaling Commission (IWC) or environmentalist agencies, in which he finds that while Inuit integrate whaling in a usage-oriented relation, the IWC and environmentalist organisations often do not (1994:123). It is within a framework of practicality that some Inuit also seem to be integrating the use of the Internet, during which its use becomes culturally valued in some concerns. The contrite inclination by some to regard Inuit and other indigenous peoples as culturally distinct groups only because of their close relationship with nature is on a collision course with the integration of advanced information and other technologies.

Cyberspace is not determined as a vacuum, whether in spatial, social, practical or mental dimensions. There is indeed coherence between the way people, not only Inuit, organise themselves in offline as well as cyberspace and thus boundary setting between groups continues, asserting as well as moving boundaries. However, rather than addressing boundaries as discriminatory or exclusive, perhaps one should instead ask whether they are not also inviting and forgiving. This would seem to be particularly pertinent regarding the attraction that Inuit cultures represent on the Web. The world we live in is not necessarily left behind by turning on the computer and looking into a screen. At least, this option seems rather far-fetched for many Inuit. Agreed, via the Internet, people can mentally go anywhere imaginable, but this is nevertheless done in the same world. Relativistic as it may sound, if Inuit are potentially affected by the Internet, they more than likely affect it as well. And if, how or when this changes is a notion that is best taken care of in futurist discussions between utopians and dystopians. But what is rather obvious is that the assertion of identity in general is subject to change by forces of time and place, for which reason Inuit identification and cultural assertion is in constant change.

IV

Perceiving Cyberspace

Cyberspace reflects a tendency to explain or metaphorise in relation to a rather ordinary and known framework – it mirrors the 'real' reality. As exemplified by the three following excerpts cyberspace was related by many Inuit Web users to practicalities within an everyday framework that represented both cyberspace and physical space, as well as offline sociality.

> "These realms [of Cyberspace] are still a little abstract and do not enter my every day even though I use e-mail and search for information via the Web." Female, Iqaluit, Nunavut, Canada (personal communication 1998).

> "Well, the Greenlandic society is a small isolated society, so cyberspace for me is a cheap way out of here. This is not meant as if I wanna get out of here, but this is the way I keep up with the latest technologies in the computer business." Male, Greenland (personal communication 1998).

> "It [cyberspace] is many things to me. On one forum that I check and contribute to regularly (http://www.nunanet.com/politics/index.html) it is a way to gauge the public's perception and see what's new in Nunavut ... it is also a great way to keep in touch with friends far away." Male, Iqaluit, Nunavut, Canada (personal communication 1998).

Abstract perceptions of cyberspace are not foreign to the participants of my research, yet the participants generally seem more ready to explain the phenomenon in regard to the immediate and practical potentials or need for the technology rather than hallucinatory mental spaces. On their Web pages, one finds a persistent wish to contextualise cyberspace within a whole world so, rather than using cyberspace to free or separate mind from matter, they use this space to create a continuum between mind and matter. Thus, a difference seems to pervade, in which Inuit explain themselves practically, whereas Euro-American theorists working within an ideological framework explain cyberspace as an abstract phenomenon. Sometimes, instead of acting in a vacuum of hallucinatory scenarios on the Web, where disembodiment is seen as a potential or a danger, some users engage and embody in the world (including cyberspace) to maintain continuity and strengthen aspects within a concoction of identity, culture, economy and political power.

In the scenario of a computer-mediated non-space where the disembodied mind is free of physical restraint, boundaries in general are not necessary or else can be bent too easily for them to exist effectively. Thus identity shifts and social as well as physical boundaries are crossed at unprecedented level to a degree where the effect of boundaries is questioned[110] – the scenario is an ambiguous anarchy in harmony. Others argue that culture is in direct opposition to technology. In this respect, technopoly – the surrender of culture to technology (Postman 1993) – stands in sharp contrast to the identity and culture affirming use of the Web discussed here. But I shall not delude myself into thinking that Inuit cannot have ideas about the Internet that precede or follow on from these perceptions. So, in preference to constructing yet another deterministic absolute of what the Internet will or will not, I acknowledge that conceptualisations of cyberspace are as varied as people's own use of the same medium.

While the polarisations of these abstract approaches take into account extremes of futurist scenarios, they do, nevertheless, seldom show much attention to the normal everyday use of the Internet. Consequently, it often disrupts the congruity between what people think could be good or bad about cyberspace and what they actually use it for. Moreover, these polarisations sustain a sensationalist image of the Internet as either culturally destructive or as a space of unlimited possibilities that pervades deeply into even the most serious research and literature. At a time where determinism has found appeal in cyberspace literature and research, as an option to grasp the vastness, fluidity, high-speed development and technological aspects of cyberspace, the practicality of these circumstances nevertheless define the medium– if I may put it this way – to be as unpredictable and as surprising as life itself.

Engaging with the world

While the Internet is often mentioned in relation to globalisation in general terms, where the ideology of a superstructural global village represents the matrix, the people encountered during this research show little interest to engage in such encapsulating rhetoric. Not that they are unaware of or uninterested in the rest of the world, but they relate to global phenomena in an overtly local/regional manner. Thus, rather than discussing global processes, homogenisation, McDonaldsization and the Internet on the basis of abstract world theory, the people who were interviewed, related to global processes through examples of local dimensions and personal experience.

The flow and mobility of culture seem to be met with an assertion that (re)locates culture to place/location – this time not only because of anthropologists, but because of how people represent themselves as well. This is evident in the content of Inuit Web pages where physicality is an eminent element by which Inuit place themselves culturally for others to see. Place thus plays an immense role in many cultures[111]. So while the possibilities of the Internet might invite people who are seeking more disembodiment in cybercultures, this separation of mind and matter is not an absolute rule in the use of cyberspace. At a time when place and culture are elements that are somehow increasingly mobile and diffuse amongst hyped anthropologists in the light of postmodernism and increasing global networking, it is nevertheless still an element that is commonly accepted amongst people as an aspect with which to assert identity and social boundaries. As Inuit live in and around the world, surf the Internet, drink Coca-Cola and watch foreign broadcasts via cable networks, they still relate their cultural identities to specific places: in relation to spaces ranging from the rest of the world, the circumpolar region, down to the space of a nucleus of relatives or friends within a specific community. This is apparent in different Web pages that take on the representation of Inuit in regard to different dimensions of location, whether it is Family Grim's home page and their identification of Aappilattoq in Upernavik, Greenland, the Taloyoak Web site; Qitsualik's Web site, or the pan-Arctic ICC Web site. The construction of Web pages are part of the processes where location continues to work as a platform to which identity is related, but it is crucial to remember that the platform used is not of static kind, but is in continuous change and both shapes as well as is shaped by the situational.

Stressing local elements of a social, physical, economic or political kind in a network with the potential for global outreach seems to confirm the old anthropological notion that culture is related to place and, in relation to the present, that Inuit exist in small secluded islands in cyberspace. However, one thing is self-representation wherein people image their habitat as self-determined and as tight-knit as possible, another is the social, political and economic relations with which Inuit are engaged in the world beyond the local dimensions whereby they define themselves:

> "The Internet gives us commonality with the rest of the world." Female, Barrow, Alaska (personal communication 1998).

> "We are not Inuit, but Inupiat, and are rapidly learning to use our connectivity to establish relationships, both personal and professional outside our immediate geographic locations." Male, Point Hope, Alaska (personal communication 1998).

My stress on the processes where language, as well as physical, mental and social boundaries seem to combine in self-referential units, should not be mistaken with the approach to culture and identity as a entity in vacuum. Indeed, as I have shown in regard to guestbooks, the assertion of boundaries lies not only in the hands of Inuit but in the hands of 'outsiders' as well and are, if not entirely unpredictable, then rather dynamic. The manifestation of local values in a global network are not distinct processes as much as the same process. Thus, rather than addressing or responding to abstract ideas of what globalisation is, the interviewees have exemplified how they interact with other individuals in other localities outside their own immediate habitat. More than anything else, this seems to be a core essence of what the Internet is and what the global process or globalisation is – communication of meaning across long and short distance between locals at an unprecedented level.

Naturally, they are aware of the forces by which local and global can interact recursively to leave a trail of continuity as well as change, but they seldom take these into account unless these forces have implications on a practical level. This not just abstract trail of continuity and change is just as well activated by people who process meaning as being primarily the practical and contextual relationships of ordinary life. While anthropologists can agree that the relationship of global and local as abstractions is a complex, which that cannot be easily explained within practicality or using only single locations – if it can be explained at all – the people they study take on the very elements of this complexity with a practical attitude that configures life to fit local ways.

Sejersen exemplifies the continuum by which Inuit have always been part of global processes. While a Western explorer by the name of Murdoch, in 1826, thought he had "found" Iñupiat in Northern Alaska, he was amazed to find these people smoking tobacco: tobacco that was likely to have been traded to Russians in Europe, then transported across Russia and Siberia to the Yup'ik in Chukotka, to end up as smoke in the throats of Iñupiat. Even more fascinating, as is commonly known, the tobacco plant had been imported to Europe in 1558 by the Portuguese from South America (1996:43-44). These elaborate trade networks similarly exist today on the Internet, where they, amongst things, help to negotiate the meaning of identity, economy and politics.

This does not imply that researchers can analyse appropriately within the same practical and local paradigm in which some Inuit present the content of the Web, but that these researchers (we) should not forget to make apparent, once in a while, that complexity is more than anything else processed through scientific approach – "The global is shallow, the local deep" (Hannerz 1996:28).

Few wish to be considered shallow and not surprisingly Inuit prefer a self image on the Web of considerable depth, entangling their identities in a mesh of significance that helps to assert Inuit as something special. Their strategy uses specificity in regard to locations of history, tradition, geography, culture, mentality, politics and economy, which provides the significance that others are looking for as they surf the Web. Being deep, regardless, does not necessarily promote complexity as much as display the shallowness that the global is prone to – put these two factors together and one has a continuous dynamic of complexity and simplicity, a thick Web of recursive actions and institutions. The Internet may be used to diffuse and assert meaning by a supposed complexity but this should not lead one to approach the subject in only abstract and global ways, nor should one dismiss the ability of people to define culture, identity and place in relation to cyberspace – in the same way that cybercultural groups identify with cyberspace as the location of their identities, Inuit identify with their locations. That cyberspace happens to be a location where Inuit reproduce, depict and assert other locations is not a peculiarity nor a sensation but an example of continuity and change.

While Inuit users may be engaged in something abstract, from a theoretical point of view, their reasons for using the Internet – as for many other users around the world – are often practical, curious or even trendy. In the polarised division of complexity and simplicity, Inuit as well as others operate within the continuum of a framework that these extremes aspire to and are inspired by – giving and taking by adding to complexity through simplicity and vice versa. The choice of whether to analyse a Web page in the light of a local or global framework is up to the analyst. The page, however, is both a product of and dependent on both elements.

Disengaging from abstract theory

My research – like all research – is an abstraction, a selected story of several selected discourses and statements that do not represent the final sum of Internet use in the Arctic. The portrait of Inuit as practical and contextual, as well as locally engaged in the use of cyberspace is a generalisation beyond doubt. Yet, as a perspective it is valid, which is why I must again stress that many Inuit are likely not to agree with some of my conclusions. I have not yet been criticised by Inuit on this account but a man from Iqaluit who is married to an Inuk woman sent me an e-mail in which he objected to what he wrongly assumed to be my intentions: "... you're likely to get responses back from Inuit that cultural content is important, but this has more to do with the fact of their inner struggle and cultural insecurities: culture and language have to be protected at all levels, even when it is unnecessary to do so." And he continues in another e-mail: "you're already assuming that the Internet even plays a key role in Inuit society, or that there is a need for it ..." (personal communication 1998).

Let me say this to clarify my intentions: the practical and culture specific use of cyberspace is not a primordial characteristic of Inuit Web use, nor is it a key factor of daily life for the majority, but it is an aspect that prevails in the use of the Internet amongst some Inuit. That I have come across these features is not solely because of my personal anthropological quest, but as much because of the many Web pages presented by Inuit and non-Inuit that deliberately try to communicate a picture of people living in certain geographical areas, with certain languages, identity and cultural traits. Yet, rather than stating this to be the way things are on an overall basis, I conclude that this is one way amongst many in which Inuit Internet users and others relate to and use cyberspace. The cultural and local specificity suggests that when Inuit engage in global networking, it is not necessarily an aspect of cultural homogenisation as much as a way of asserting elements such as local identity, economy and political power or simply pure entertainment. The attitude of many participants towards cyberspace was generally utilitarian rather than abstract, but I cannot say that all were alike. As argued by Hannerz, people relate differently to 'world culture', a concept that does not infer "a replication of uniformity, but an organisation of diversity, an increasing interconnectedness of varied local cultures" (1996:102). While Inuit might relate more locally or globally to global process they do so in relation to the character of situations – not that every action taken is either latently grounded in their culture or that they have been taken over by the network. Sometimes Inuit We users act as global citizens and at other times as locals.

I do not wish to promote yet another determinist approach to how groups of people act in cyberspace. Because the possibility exists of becoming a part-time cyborg or engaging in a mental and hallucinatory non-space, people can still choose not to discard their local culture as well as not to: it still holds that social or symbolic boundaries can be crossed; that people are not solely characterised by the traits of their culture, but by the way they organise themselves. Thus, an Inuk who is Web master for a specific cultural or 'local' Web site is not solely characterised by this parameter. There are other situations in which he or she is likely to create a different self-image and engage in social boundaries that may be believed to be hallucinatory, disembodied or cybercultural. I have merely investigated those boundaries that surround cultural identities. Nowhere in my research for this book have I assumed that the Internet plays a key role in Inuit societies or that there is a major need for it, nor do the responses from Inuit Web users suggest such an overwhelming trend. What I have done, is to recognise the cultural and social perspectives of boundary maintenance that, nevertheless, are manifested globally on the Web by Inuit users and those who visit their Web pages. The offline effects in the local setting of this online boundary maintenance have not been part of my research for reasons discussed in the chapter on methodology[112].

Originally, I was interested in investigating how Inuit use the Internet and then in developing research from what I found. As stated earlier, the cultural focus on local and regional manifestations on a global network only emerged slowly during research. Partly because it interested me and partly because I could see it happening before my eyes – as well as having this observation supported by the statements of Inuit Web users. It adds one example to the existing body of knowledge that local identities and cultures are dynamic and manifest in social networks that are not self-sustained local vacuums but which are processed in a complex network of social relations that include the global process. The complexity or banality of processing identity might seldom be one we think about on a daily basis. An abstract discussion about non-space or transcendence very occasionally emerged from my interviews, as much as Inuit were keen to 'talk' about utilising cyberspace to support and develop the Arctic. Yet, while localism and peripherality still seem deeply embedded in their conceptions of being part of a global network, their use of the Internet – but not an exclusive use – strengthened locality and their sense of belonging. Where the 1980s and 1990s witnessed the emergent idea of thinking globally and acting locally –

mostly in regard to environmental issues (see Sejersen 1998:242) – this sort of Internet use rather seems to connote the idea of thinking locally and acting globally[113].

Continuity? Accept Change and understand Context

Mobility and change of identities and cultures does not necessitate deep sixing already existing cultural identities. Nor does the imagined compression of space render local identities redundant: rather the contrary. A sense of belonging is as mobile as the people who manifest and negotiate its many meanings. Social and cultural change has always existed but it is becoming more rapid, analogue to a worldwide increase in communication. One should remember, however, that rapid change and cyberspace are not self-sustained organisms but processes driven by people. Technological determinism in regard to what the Internet will or will not do fails to address what people do. The basic premise is that the Internet does nothing without people. Change of social boundaries and cultural content is not so much a conflict as an integral to constantly developing processes of identification, i.e. human interaction. It seems that the more we compress the imagined sense of space and time, the faster change occurs. And so communication and human interaction lie at the very heart of rapid change.

In this respect, it is interesting that much research into communication and media focuses on discontinuous processes: many do not seem to approach the combined context of offline and online in regard to the Internet. Accordingly, it could seem that we do not deal enough with the everyday and practical context of the occurring changes, an approach basically associated with continuity, but emphasise the extremes of change by digging for conflicts and sensations. Contemporary postmodernist research almost seems obsessed with discontinuity and fragmentation. True, this book is obsessed with continuity, but it does not claim the full picture. It merely documents and discusses some of those instances where continuity is actively pursued by Inuit; where changing livelihood is not necessarily discontinuous, but continuous. This line of thinking is partly a reaction towards the tendency to stigmatise Inuit cultures and societies as static traditional hunter-gatherer cultures, latently in conflict with contemporary society. This deduction that is far too simplistic. Inuit cultures and social boundaries are simultaneously modern and traditional, similar to all other living cultures with histories of their own. Suicide, abuse and unemployment are not simple conflicts between tradition and modernism but are much more socially and economically intricate.

Even though offline social organisation may seem more static to the naked eye, compared to the possibilities of shifting between a multitude of individual identities in a chat room, they nevertheless deal with the dynamics of the same world. Extremes provide the sensations, while users provide the common and continual exchange of meanings that, amongst other things, are used to shape identity and culture on a daily basis. In the opinion of Featherstone: identity formation and "the once secure fantasy based on 'we and they' images" has enabled categories of people "with more fluid identities" (1995: 154). Jenkins notes that while the speed for the greater opportunity for differentiation has been increased by new modes of communication have, differentiation itself is not a radically new phenomenon – it simply *is* (1997:50).

I started out with the objective of investigating the processes wherein Inuit and others negotiate social boundaries, culture and identity. In the course of analysis, it became clear that even transcendence, supposedly making the notion of physicality evaporate into cyberspace, has a hard time finding itself – being thoroughly displaced by the content as well as the social interaction of many Web pages. That there are abundant amounts of boundary assertion, socially, physically as well as mentally, is beyond reasonable doubt. Pictures, photographs, art galleries, pages with Inuit history and their relation to the land, and much more, all serve as platforms to identify local and cultural identities. By constructing these pages in specific ways, on-lookers, whether or not they are Inuit, relate to the value of the Web page with a sense of belonging or its opposite. Within this multi-referential process where one situates the 'self' in relation to the space/place visited, the notion of social boundaries emerges. Thus, some Inuit pre-empt the supposed emptiness of transnationality or globalisation (where belonging to locations becomes somewhat diffuse) by presenting themselves on Web pages. The use of technology to process this assertion of self is no paradox, nor is it a usage that makes Inuit less Inuit, unless they themselves believe it to be so. In the contemporary world, culture may still be associated to place but it is not dependent on a fixed space to be spatial.

Obviously, one cannot ignore that the affirmation of identity is done differently in different spaces: something rather natural to the situational nature of identities, I may add. In this respect, the scenario of a secluded and boundary free cyberspace, motioned as a result of Internet usage by Euro-American males[114] from the wealthier parts of society in the 1980s and early 1990s, seems a universal concept so narrow, brittle and moribund that one cannot blame these enthusiasts for running away from home to live in their secure realm of cyberspace. Hence, in regard to conceptions and use of cyberspace, what might have been the case in the 1980s has been altered elsewhere by changes in the utilisation of the Internet: if not dramatically then remarkably. The case of the Arctic presents one such example. Changes are brought about by the use of the Internet but Internet usage, too, is also subject to change.

As the relationship of culture and place has shifted its paradigm within anthropological theory to a point of less determinism between the two, this has been done with an understanding of what the world looks and feels like. This shift has been achieved not just in relation to local culture, but just as well to the surrounding world that both helps to define and be defined by local culture. Because culture has become more transitory and is now negotiated in other corners of the world than previously, it still *is*. The entry into the age of hallucinatory cyberspace, however, seems to have produced the idea that certain cultures, in this case members of transcendent cybercultures, are the only real inhabitants of computer-mediated space, while at the same time claiming non-space to be a non-cultural space open to all people. No matter how I twist and turn it, this idea assumes that a certain transcendent culture or non culture is associated with a certain space. While this link between culture and place is perfectly valid on the part of users who believe in it, we know from an anthropological point of view that culture may be associated with certain places but it is not necessarily dependent on these – paradoxically part of the non-space argument as well. Thus, Inuit presence in cyberspace is not automatically a starting point for their own cultural extinction. Some Inuit still embed their local identity and culture despite all the fragmentation and disembodiment reported in postmodern literature. For this and other reasons, we might want to consider fragmentation more as a process of cultural diversification rather than singularisation. I have tried to negotiate the extremes by which much sensationalist and futurist literature partakes in defining the combined elements of culture, identity and cyberspace. In response to these extremes, where all-encompassing ideology starts and practicality ceases, the aspects of Internet usage where Inuit assert their offline culture and identity have proven essential, to supply the missing continuum between online and offline that these theoretical extremes have helped to remove. While such extremes of polarised meaning may provide important contributions, they seem to bear little similarity with contemporary practice.

As I have tried to show, some Inuit assert their cultural, local, ethnic, national and personal identities and, although it puts them in direct contact with people far away at an unprecedented level, one cannot predict what this will mean in the future. The majority of Web users that I corresponded with for several months during my online fieldwork seem to think of the Web as a potential rather than a threat. As for now, their cultures and identities are dynamically asserted every minute on the Web and in ways partly defined by themselves. The right to self-determination that has been difficult to get in physical space[115] seems to have come easy in cyberspace. Nevertheless, one should not mistake that the main reason for this is that people do not live continuously in cyberspace. Most of the time, at least, Inuit users turn off the computers and engage offline. Thus, self-determination for Inuit in cyberspace means little without the same rights in physical space.

"Stressing local elements of a social, physical, economic or political kind in a network with the potential for global outreach seems to confirm the old anthropological notion that culture is related to place and, in relation to the present, that Inuit exist in small secluded islands in cyberspace. However, one thing is self-representation wherein people image their habitat as self-determined and as tight-knit as possible, another is the social, political and economic relations with which Inuit are engaged in the world beyond the local dimensions whereby they define themselves."

I would like to finish by both repeating an earlier paragraph from this work and by citing the words of three Inuit Web users:

> "... people outside the Arctic will have a better understanding of the people who live in the Arctic and do away with a lot of the misconceptions made by those 'outside'." Female, Nome, Alaska (personal communication 1998).

> "I hope that the Internet can bring people from different cultures together efficiently." Female, Happy Valley, Labrador, Canada (personal communication 1998).

> "We've got to stick together to survive, and we need to use all possible and peaceful means to achieve this end." Male, Nuuk, Greenland (personal communication 1998).

Appendix

Survey results
Questionnaire

	Options	%
1. Name:		
2. Gender:	**Male**	**57**
	Female	43
3. Age:	**(average age, not %)**	**34**
4. I live in (country, region, community):	**Canada**	**37**
	Greenland	22
	Alaska	35
	other place	6
5. I started using the Internet (year):	**(average year, not %)**	**1994**
6. I use the Internet for:	**e-mail**	**30**
	surfing	**30**
	presentation	24
	work	16
	other	-
7. I connect from:	**home**	**43**
	work	39
	access centre	4
	school	14
	other	-
8. I mostly connect to:	Arctic	17
	outside Arctic	**83**

9. I believe Internet changes the Arctic:	**yes**	**86**
	no	8
	don't know	6
10. I have established contacts outside the Arctic through the use of through the use of Internet:	**yes**	**81**
	no	19
11. Who gains the most from Internet:	**individual**	**46**
	corporation	17
	organisation	6
	communities	31
12. I believe that one category's success will benefit the others:	**yes**	**66**
	no	2
	don't know	22
13. Development of Internet should be promoted through:	private entrepeneurship	18
	government	7
	partnership	**75**
14. Information highway brings	world into Arctic	18
	Arctic into world	11
	both ways equel	**71**
15. Cultural contents are important on Arctic Web pages:	**yes**	**71**
	no	14
	don't know	15
16. Internet brings development to the Arctic:	**yes**	**60**
	no	20
	don't know	20

17. I think the Internet effect:	promotes culture	40
	promotes business	**43**
	is overrated	17

18. I think the Internet makes us all alike:	yes	28
	no	**58**
	don't know	14

19. People will gain more independence from a central form of government through use of Internet:	yes	29
	no	**48**
	don't know	14

20. Internet will bring people in the entire Arctic closer together:	**yes**	**54**
	no	30
	don't know	16

21. What are your major concerns or hope for what Internet will bring in the future

22. Any other comments

Notes

Introduction: Shifting Boundaries

1. The Web pages of the Rankin Inlet league: [Web page] URL http://www.nunavut.nu/hockey/info.html [visit: February 20, 1999].
2. The World Wide Web (the Web) originated around 1990 with the use of Hyper-Text Markup Language (HTML). In 1994, the W3C (The World Wide Web Consortium) was founded to implement common protocols. Since then the use of the medium has seen an increasing development. Dushin has given an excellent account on the conventions and history of the Web (Dushin 1998). For a general history of the Internet see Cerf & Aboba 1993 or Rheingold 1993.
3. For a broad selection of literature dealing with disembodiment please consult Curtis 1996, Hamman 1996, Lyon 1997, North 1994, Reid 1991, Rheingold 1993 and Turkle 1984 and 1995.
4. By offline culture I refer to culture that is not dependent on cyberspace for its existence but which nevertheless may still be manifested and reproduced in cyberspace as well as outside. Although this sort of polarised reference goes against the object of clarifying the continuum created between online and offline, it is needed to argue the greater outline of my approach.
5. A number of perspectives in regard to social and cultural dynamics are discussed and exemplified by Barth 1969, Dahl 1986, Dorais 1997, Fienup-Riordan 1990, ICC 1992, Kleivan 1969/70, Oosten & Remie 1999, Pullar 1992 and Sejersen 1996.
6. The word Eskimo may sound derogatory to Inuit, while not necessarily to others such as the Yup'ik Eskimos, or Iñupiat. I experienced several Inuit Web users from Canada who were not happy about the name of my University Department (Dept. of Eskimology). The distinctions of the term has also been discussed in different UseNet groups by Inuit as well as Eskimos. I will mostly use the term Inuit as used by the ICC, thus emphasising a political meaning, rather than disregarding the diversity of cultural identities in the Arctic. See Burch 1988 for a discussion.
7. Nunavik is located in Arctic Québec.
8. The paragraphed statements that appear throughout the book come from my online fieldwork, carried out throughout most of 1998. See chapter two for the methodology of this fieldwork.
9. Please consult the Dahl 1989 and 1993, Oosten & Remie 1999, Sejersen 1994 and Wenzel 1986 for discussion on modernity and hunting.
10. The Qitsualik Web site is an example: [Web site] URL http://www.cyberus.ca/~stinsley/qit.htm [visit: July 18, 1999].
11. Please consult Dahl 1993, ICC 1992 and Sambo 1992 for discussions on the need for self-determination.
12. For examples of Arctic Internet studies please consult Alia 1999, Hansen 1998 and 1999, Hayden 1999, Inuit Broadcasting Company 1994, Pedersen 1998, Stenbæk 1998a and 1998b and Zellen 1998.
13. MUD (Multi User Dimension or Dungeon) is a platform for engaging in networked games or social interaction of different sort. For more information please consult Curtis 1996. MOO (MUD Object oriented) entails more use of graphics.

14. There is an abundance of interesting studies. See for instance Coon 1998, Curtis 1996, Hamman 1998 and Reid 1991 and 1994.
15. For a discussion of difference, local diversity or pan-Arctic unification consult Dybbroe 1991; Fienup-Riordan 1990, Hensel 1996 and ICC 1992.

I Going Nowhere to get Everywhere

16. Please consult Bernard 1988 and Ellen 1984 for a discussion of anthropological method.
17. Personal communication with Sejersen in 1999.
18. This goes for the 70 people who originally supplied me with their e-mail addresses in the online pilot survey as well as others who have been interviewees – such as Web masters – all of whom have access to the World Wide Web. In a few cases the papers have been sent as e-mail attachments for those with slow network connections and expensive long distance charges.
19. [Web page] URL http://www.greennet.gl [visit: May 26, 1999]
20. The ratio of men and women in interviews has been at an average of 60-40. In the 1998 pilot survey the ratio was 57% male and 43% female respondents.
21. See Christensen 1998.
22. For examples of this participatory method please consult Dahl 1989 Hensel 1996, Sejersen 1998 and Wenzel 1986.
23. [Web site] URL http://home.worldonline.dk/~nbc/ [visit: July 14, 2000]
24. Olwig & Hastrup discuss the changing dynamics of fieldwork and method (Olwig & Hastrup 1997:8).
25. The address was later changed and finally replaced by http://home.worldonline.dk/~nbc/.
26. The perspectives of the survey results are discussed in *Inuit in Cyberspace: Arctic users networking between past and future* (Christensen 1998).
27. Please consult Berthelsen 1976 for further information on the newspaper debate.
28. Audio-visual videoconferencing equipment or Web cams could be used but I doubt that the effect would be one similar to face-to-face contact.
29. As a note to the analysis of Web pages, and specifically guestbooks, I have attempted to get consent from the authors' of entries. However, some of the e-mail addresses are either false or outdated, which has hindered contact. If anyone takes offence at this, I apologise and argue that the entries in the guest-books are public and can be quoted when using adequate reference. In this book I have chosen to erase the names of the guestbook authors, but maintain a reference to the location on the Web where the original entries can be found.
30. Please consult Waskul 1996 and Reid 1996 in regard to the ethical dilemmas attached to research in MUD and MOO.
31. Please consult Chandler 1998, Crowston & Williams 1997 and 1999 and Walters 1996.

II (Re)producing the Arctic in Cyberspace

32. [Web site] URL http://www.geocities.com/Athens/Thebes/4632/ [visit: July 22, 2000]
33. Gemeinschaft/ Gesellschaft was first addressed by Toennies (Toennies (1957)[1887]) who used it to differ between rural and urban life. Gemeinschaft was associated with social relations in homogeneous small-scale networks, while

Gesellschaft was more impersonal, contractual and ran parallel to the individualism of modern/urban population centres. See Pahl 1965 for a discussion of their meaning in an urban/rural perspective.
34. Please consult Gates 1996, Haraway 1985, Lanier 1990, Negroponte 1995, Rheingold 1993, Springer 1991 and Toffler 1980.
35. Please consult Haraway 1985, Lanier 1990 and Springer 1991.
36. Please consult Dery 1997, Postman 1993, Robins 1995 and Schiller 1993.
37. Removed for matters of confidence.
38. The selected paragraph is often used by utopians to define cyberspace. Nevertheless, the book itself contains a quite pessimistic view on future technology and society.
39. Instead of writing about rural environment, Gurstein writes about a "Non-Metropolitan Environment". He defines the Metropolitan environment as one where intellectual, financial and physical resources are concentrated and where there is a significant density of population and activity, which again supports specialised activities that are focal for financial, economic and intellectual creativity (Gurstein 1998: paragraph 6). It is within such a paradigm covering social, geographical, political and economical aspects that this paper refers to rurality.
40. For an interesting discussion on the complexities of this theme in relation to the Highlands and Islands of Scotland see Black, Bryden and Sproull 1996.
41. [Web document] URL http://www.canarie.ca [visit: November 24, 1998]
42. [Web site] URL http://www.asrc.com [visit: July 25: 1999]
43. [Web site] URL http://www.arcticworld.com [visit: July 25, 1999]
44. [Web site] URL http://www.asna.org [visit: July 25, 1999]
45. See the Web site of the Food and Agriculture Organisation, United Nations (FAO), [Web site] URL http://www.fao.org [visit: July 25, 1999], the Web site of the World Bank, [Web site] URL http://www.worldbank.org [visit: July 25, 1999], or the Web site for the United Nations Research Institute for Social Development (UNRISD), [Web site] URL http://www.unrisd.org/ [visit: July 25, 1999].
46. ARDICOM has its network hub in Yellowknife, but has yet another hub planned in Iqaluit, the capitol of Nunavut, as well. The network runs through satellite channels and digital microwave where it is available. All depending on community size they can offer network speeds to ISPs from T1 to 64k. Northwestel, NASCo and ACL each own 1/3.
47. [Web document] URL http://www.ssimicro.com.al.html [visit: April 23, 1999]
48. CAP is a federal government initiative that provides grants for Internet access in remote and rural communities of Canada. Funding is usually between $4,000 and $18,000 US per grant with a maximum of $25,000. Hayden's thesis on the effect of the CAP site in Rankin Inlet states that respondents did not note positive impact in areas such as democracy, community building, environmental or societal impact as much as they noted a positive impact in personal efficacy (1999:41). A result that is similar to my findings from the online survey.
49. [Web document] URL http://www.schoolnet.ca/home/e/ [visit: April 23, 1999]
50. [Web site] URL http://www.nortext.com [visit: July 24, 1999]
51. [Web site] URL http://www.arctic-travel.com [visit: July 25, 1999]
52. [Web site] URL http://www.nunavut.com [visit: July 21, 1999]
53. Although, it was not until late 1997 that the network connecting the different parts of the country and the surrounding world were also fully digitised. Until then, only the local networks had been digitised.
54. The Greenlandic Home Rule is the major shareholder of Tele Greenland.

55. [Web site] URL http://www.greenland-guide.gl/aul/default.htm [visit: July 25, 1999]
56. [Web site] URL http://www.qamutitexpress.com/ [visit: July 25, 1999]
57. [Web site] URL http://www.alaska.net [visit: July 25, 1999]
58. [Web site] URL http://www.alyeska-pipe.com [visit: July 25, 1999]
59. For qualification schools must have no less than 10 students and be without an existing connection. The money only for connecting the schools. It is the responsibility of the schools themselves to fund or otherwise attain funding for the computer equipment.
60. [Web site] URL http://www.nsbsd.k12.ak.us [visit: July 25, 1999]
61. See for instance Talero & Gaudette 1996 and The Information Highway Advisory Council 1995.

III A Common Web of Difference and Similarity

62. For a similar discussion, please consult Dybbroe, who discusses the value of culture in social interaction (Dybbroe 1996: 41).
63. He has later re-developed his ideas during the 1990s, and carefully included the importance of individuality and content in combination with social organisation – see for instance Barth 1994.
64. [Web site] URL http://www.nunanet.com/~arctic/ [visit: July 30, 1999]
65. [Web site] URL http://iserit.greennet.gl/inussuk/ [visit: July 30, 1999]
66. [Web site] URL http://www.uqqurmiut.com/print97.htm/ [visit: July 31, 1999]
67. See for instance Levi Palutiq Outfitting, [Web site] URL http://www. nunanet.com/~palituq/ [visit: July 30, 1999] or Greenland Guide, [Web site] http://www.greenland-guide.dk/ [visit: July 31, 1999].
68. [Web site] URL http://www.polarnet.ca/~taloyoak/information/ [visit: July 31, 1999]
69. [Web site] URL http://www.polarnet.ca/~taloyoak/ [visit: July 31, 1999]
70. See Balikci 1970 for a comprehensive ethnography of the Netsilingmiut – the local Inuit.
71. [Web document] URL http://cnet.unb.ca/cap [visit: December 4, 1998]
72. [Web site] URL http://www.arctic.ca/LUS/CAC.html [visit: July 29, 1999]
73. [Web site] URL http://www.ssimicro.com/~arviat/ [visit: July 29, 1999]
74. [Web site] URL http://www.polarnet.ca/~netsilik/ [visit: July 31, 1999]
75. [Web page] URL http://www.polarnet.ca/~taloyoak/taloyoak.htm [visit: July 31, 1999]
76. [Web site] URL http://www.polarnet.ca/ [visit: July 31, 1999]
77. [Web site] URL http://www.arctic-can.nt.ca/taluq/pages/map1.htm [visit: July 31, 1999]
78. [Web site] URL http://www.firstair.ca/ [visit: July 31, 1999]
79. Taloyoak Information page links to the Nunavut Tourist Guide for information.
80. [Web page] URL http://www.polarnet.ca/~taloyoak/information/Whitepages.htm [visit: July 31, 1999]
81. [Web page] URL http://www.polarnet.ca/~taloyoak/information/Whoswho.htm [visit: July 31, 1999]
82. [Web site] URL http://www.nuuk.gl/ [visit: July 31, 1999]
83. [Web site] URL http://iserit.greennet.gl/qaanaaq/ [visit: July 31, 1999]
84. [Web site] URL http://www.nsbsd.k12.ak.us/NUIWEB/inter2.htm/ [visit: July, 31, 1999]

85. [Web site] URL http://www.nsbsd.k12.ak.us/BTIWEB/Main.html] [visit: July, 31, 1999]
86. [Web site] URL http://www.pail.ca/ [visit: July 31, 1999]
87. [Web site] URL http://iserit.greennet.gl/ilutrade/ [visit: July 31, 1999]
88. [Web site] URL http://www.kodiak.org/ [visit: July 31, 1999]
89. [Web site] URL http://www.inuusiat.org/ [visit: July 31, 1999]
90. Search carried out December 11, 1998, at [Web site] http://www.altavista.digital.com.
91. [Web site] URL http://www.cyberus.ca/~stinsley/qit.htm/ [visit: July 31, 1999]
92. [Web site] URL http://www.piteraq.gl/ [visit: July 31, 1999]
93. Greenlandic in this case refers to the all the dialects in Greenland.
94. [Web site] URL http://www.nunavut.com [visit: July 26, 1999]
95. [Web site] URL http://www.nunatsiaq. com [visit: July 26, 1999]
96. [Web site] URL http://www.avataq.qc.ca [visit: July 26, 1999]
97. [Web site] URL http://www.ssimicro.com/~arviat/ [visit: July 26, 1999]
98. [Web site] URL http://www.qikiqtaalukcorp.nu.ca [visit: July 26, 1999]
99. [Web site] URL http://www.nunanet.com/~lands/ [visit: July 26, 1999]
100. [Web site] URL http://www.makivik.org [visit: July 26, 1999)
101. It is not always possible to decipher from the text whether people address family or friends. However, it is quite obvious that they refer to social relations within a given community or socio-sphere.
102. When using words such as "global" and "worldwide" one should be aware that it is documented by the ITU/BDT Telecommunication Indicator Database, that as much as half the global population have never used a telephone (Hamelink 1997:18).
103. [Web page] URL http://iserit.greennet.gl/grillen/ [visit: June 23, 2000]
104. [Web page] URL http://www.nsbsd.k12.ak.us/anaktuvuk/akpWeb/akpinter/akpinter.htm [visit: June 24, 2000]
105. [Web page] URL http://www.polarnet.ca/polarnet/kia.htm [visit: June 23, 2000]
106. [Web page] URL http://www.makivik.org [visit: June 23, 2000]
107. [Web page] URL http://www.gh.gl [visit: June 23, 2000]
108. [Web page] URL http://www.inusiaat.com/ [visit: June 23, 2000]
109. For discussions on the consequences of modernity please consult Dahl 1986, Dorais 1997, Hensel 1996, Kleivan 1969 and 1970 and Nuttall 1992.

IV Perceiving Cyberspace

110. If a person has become unpopular in a chat room, often all that is needed is for the person to leave and re-enter under a different name and a different attitude. The social boundaries that exist amongst the sub-groups of people within the space can thus be crossed and violated again and again by use of ordinary social skill.
111. As earlier mentioned, please consult Dybbroe 1991 and Nuttall 1992 for some interesting discussions on the meaning of place and community.
112. For perspectives on the offline effects please consult Hayden 1999, in which he investigates the effects of the Rankin Inlet CAP access centre, *Igalaaq*, in Nunavut, or Hansen 1999, in which similarly the use of an access centre in Innaarsuit, Greenland, is investigated.
113. I wish to thank Frank Sejersen for bringing my attention to this difference in strategies.

Continuity? Accept Change and Understand Context

114. In regard to Yup'ik identity and gender, Hensel makes a note of the differences in highlighting aspects of men's and women's identity by an unequal affect by Western development (1996:15). Lack of space prevents discussing the gender-issue relating to the Internet, but please note that most Arctic Web pages are currently mastered by men.
115. Please consult Asch 1992, Berger 1985 and Dahl 1988 for discussions on the struggle for self-determination in the Arctic.

References

Agre, Phil (1999), 'Life After Cyberspace', in *Red Rock Eater News Service (RRE)*, Sunday April 11

Alia, Valerie (1999), *Un/covering the North*. Vancouver, UBC Press

Asch, Michael (1992), 'Political self-sufficiency', pp. 45-52, in *Nation to Nation: Aboriginal sovereignty and the future of Canada*, D. Engelstadt and J. Bird, eds. Concord, Anasi Press

Balikci, Asen (1970), *The Netsilik Eskimo*. Garden City, New York, The Natural History Press

Barglow, Raymond (1994), *The Crisis of the Self in the Age of Information: Computers, Dolphins and Dreams*. London, Routledge

Barlow, John Perry (1996), *A Declaration of the Independence of Cyberspace*. [WWW doc.] URL http://www.eff.org/pub/Publications/John_Perry_ Barlow /barlow_0296.declaration. [Visit: November 22, 1998]

Barth, Fredrik (1969), 'Introduction', pp. 9-38 in *Ethnic Groups and Boundaries: The Social Organization of Culture Difference*, F. Barth, ed. Oslo, Universitetsforlaget

Barth, Fredrik (1994), *Manifestasjon og process*. Oslo, Universitetsforlaget

Baudrillard, Jean (1993), 'Xerox og det uendelige', in *Kulturens Digitale Felt: Essays om informasjonsteknologiens betydning*, T. Rasmussen & M. Søby, eds. Oslo, Aventura Forlag A/S

Bauman, Zygmunt (1998), *Globalisation: The Human Consequences*. Cambridge, Polity Press

Benedikt, Michael (1991), 'Introduction', in *Cyberspace: First Steps*, M. Benedikt, ed. Cambridge, MA, MIT Press

Berger, John (1995), *Ways of Seeing*. London, BBC & Penguin Books

Berger, Thomas R. (1985), *Village Journey – the Report of the Alaska Native Review Commission*. New York, Hill & Wang

Bernard, H. Russel (1988), *Research Methods in Cultural Anthropology*. London, Sage

Berthelsen, Christian (1976) *Det at være Grønlænder: Fra en debat i begyndelsen af det 20. Århundrede*. The periodical *Grønland*, 4: 117-121

Black, Stuart and John Bryden, Alan Sproull (1996), 'Telematics, rural economic development and SMEs: Some demand-side evidence', in *Informationen zur Raumentwiklung*, 11/12: 755-775

Bollman, Ray D. (1994), 'A Preliminary Typology of Rural Canada', pp. 141-144, in *Towards Sustainable Rural Communities*, J. M. Bryden, ed. The Guelph Seminar Series

Burch Jr., Ernest S. (1988), *The Eskimos*. London, Macdonald Orbis

Cerf, Vinto & Bernard Aboba (1993) 'How the Internet Came to Be', by Vinton Cerf, as told to Bernard Aboba in *The Online User's Encyclopedia*. Reading Mass., Addison-Wesley

Chance, Norman A. (1990), *The Iñupiat and Arctic Alaska: An Ethnography of Development*. Fort Worth, Tex., Holt, Rinehart and Winston

Chandler, Daniel (1997a), *Introduction to Genre Theory*. [WWW doc.] URL http://www.aber.ac.uk/~dgc/intgenre.html [Visit: July 20, 1999]

Chandler, Daniel (1997b), *Writing Oneself in Cyberspace*. [WWW doc.] URL http://www.aber.ac.uk/~dgc/homepgid.html [Visit: July 20, 1999]

Chandler, Daniel (1998), *Personal Home Pages and the Construction of Identities on the Web*. Paper presented at Linking Theory and Practice: Issues in the Politics of Identity conference, September 9-11, 1998. The Aberystwyth Post-International Group, University of Wales. [WWW doc.] URL http://www.aber.ac.uk/~dgc/Webident.html [Visit: July 20, 1999]

Christensen, Neil Blair (1998), *Inuit in Cyberspace: Arctic users networking between past and future*. Paper presented at the 11th Inuit Studies Conference, 21-28 September, Nuuk

Clark, Grahame (1992), *Space, Time and Man: A Prehistorian's View*. Cambridge, Cambridge University Press

Cohen, Anthony P. (1985), *The Symbolic Construction of Community*. London, Tavistock

Cohen, Anthony P. (1986) 'Of Symbols and Boundaries, or does Ertie's Greatcoat hold the Key?', pp. 1-19 in *Symbolising Boundaries: Identity and Diversity in British Cultures*, A. P. Cohen, ed. Manchester University Press

Coomber, R. (1997), 'Using the Internet for Survey Research', in *Sociological Research Online*, 2(2). [WWW doc.] URL http://www.socresonline.org.uk/socresonline/2/2/2.html [Visit: December 5, 1998]

Coon, David Alan (1998), *An investigation of #Friends Internet Relay Chat*. MA Thesis, Southeastern Louisiana University

Crowston, K & M. Williams (1997), *Reproduced and emergent genres of communication on the World-Wide Web.* Paper presented at HICSS-97, Kilea, Hawaii, January 1997. [WWW doc.] URL http://florin.syr.edu/~crowston/papers/Webgenres.html [Visit: July 20, 1999]

Crowston, K & M. Williams (1999), *The Effects of Linking on Genres of Web Documents.* Paper to appear at HICSS-99, Kilea, Hawaii, January 1999. [WWW doc.] URL http://florin.syr.edu/~crowston/papers/ddgen 04.html [Visit: July 20, 1999]

Curtis, Pavel (1996), 'Mudding: Social Phenomena in Text-Based Virtual Realities', pp. 265-292 in *Internet Dreams. Archetypes, Myths, and Metaphors*, M. Stefik. Cambridge, Mass., MIT Press

Dahl, Jens (1986), 'Udviklingsaspektet i kulturen', *Stofskifte* 14: 13-25

Dahl, Jens (1988), 'Self-Government, Land Claims and Imagined Inuit Communities' in *FOLK* 30: 73-84

Dahl, Jens (1989), 'The Integrative and Cultural Role of Hunting and Subsistence in Greenland', in *Études/Inuit/Studies*, 13(1): 23-42

Dahl, Jens (1993), 'Indigenous Peoples of the Arctic', pp. 103-127, in *NORD, Arctic Challenges*. Stockholm: The Nordic Council

Dery, Mark (1997), *Escape Velocity – Cyberculture at the End of the Century.* London, Hodder & Stoughton General

De Santis, Solange (1998), 'Across Tundra and Cultures, Entrepreneur Wires Arctic', in *The Wall Street Journal*, October 19: B1 & B5

Dorais, Louis Jacques (1991), 'Language, Identity and Integration in the Canadian Arctic', *North Atlantic Studies*, 3(1): 18-24

Dorais, Louis-Jacques (1995/96), 'Inuugatta inuulerpugut: Kalaallit and Canadian identities', pp. 28-33 in *Grønlandsk Kultur- og Samfunds-forskning 95*. Nuuk, Atuakkiorfik

Dorais, Louis Jacques (1997), *Quaqtaq; Modernity and Identity in an Inuit Community*. Toronto, University of Toronto Press

Dushin, Megan (1998), *Evolution of Conventions on the World Wide Web*. [WWW doc.] URL http://www.ici.coled.umn.edu/megs/conventions.html [Visit: December 10, 1998]

Dybbroe, Susanne (1991), 'Local Organisation and Cultural Identity in Greenland in a National Perspective', *North Atlantic Studies* 3(1): 5-17

Dybbroe, Susanne (1996), 'Questions of Identity and issues of self-determination', in *Études/Inuit/Studies* 20(2): 39-53

Ellen, R.F. (1984), *Ethnographic Research: A Guide to General Conduct*. London, Harcourt Brace & Company

Eriksen, Thomas Hylland (1991), 'The Cultural Contexts of Ethnic Differences', *Man* 26(1). [WWW doc.] URL http://www.sv.uio.no/~geirthe/Culturalcontexts.html [Visit: December 10, 1998]

Erickson, Thomas (1996), *The World Wide Web as Social Hypertext*. [WWW doc.] URL http://www.pliant.org/personal/Tom_Erickson/SocialHypertext.html [Visit: December 10, 1998].

Escobar, Arturo (1994), 'Welcome to Cyberia: Notes on the Anthology of Cyberculture', in *Current Anthropology* 35(3): 211-232

Featherstone, Mike (1995), *Undoing Culture: Globalisation, Postmodernism and Identity*. London, Sage

Featherstone, Mike & Roger Burrows (1995), *Cyberspace/Cyberbodies/Cyberpunk: Cultures of Technological Embodiment*, M. Featherstone & R. Burrows, eds. London, Sage

Fienup-Riordan, Ann (1990), *Eskimo Essays: Yup'ik lives and how we see them*. New Brunswick, Rutgers University Press

Fortescue, Michael (1998), *Language relations across Bering Strait*. London, Cassell

Friedman, Jonathan (1990), 'Being in the World: Globalisation and Localisation', pp. 311-328, in *Global Culture: Nationalism, Globalisation and Modernity. A Theory, Culture & Society special issue*, M. Featherstone, ed. London, Sage in association with Theory, culture & society

Friedman, Jonathan (1994), *Cultural Identity & Global Process*. London, Sage

Friedman, Jonathan (1995), 'Global System, Globalisation, and the Parameters of Modernity', pp. 69-90, in *Global Modernities*, M. Featherstone, ed. London, Sage

Gates, Bill (1996), *The Road Ahead*. London, Viking

Gibson, William (1995 [1984]), *Neuromancer*. London, Voyager, Harper Collins Publishers

Graburn, Nelson H. (1982), 'Television and the Canadian Inuit', in *Etudes/Inuit/Studies* 6(1): 39-48

Grønlands Hjemmestyre (1996), *Grønland og Informationssamfundet, Elementer i en informationsteknologisk strategi*. Nuuk, Landsstyrets IT-arbejdsgruppe

Grønlands Hjemmestyre (1997), *IT-politisk redegørelse*. Nuuk, Direktoratet for Erhverv, Traffik og Forsyning (FM 1997/DETF 34.91+1)

Grønlands IT-Råd (2000), *Vi bygger en nation. Grønlands muligheder i internet-samfundet*. Nuuk

Grønlands Radioavis (1999a), *IT-råd foreslår sponsorering af computere*, writeout from May 25

Grønlands Radioavis (1999b), *Ny afregningsmodel for internettet*, writeout from June 7

Gurstein, Michael (1998), *Using Information and Communications Technology for Local Economic Development in a Non-Metropolitan Environment*. [WWW doc.] URL http://www. fao.org [Visit: November 10,1998]

Hamelink, Cees J. (1997), *New Information and Communication Technologies, Social Development and Cultural Change*, in United Nations Research Institute for Social Development (UNRISD), Discussion Paper no. 86

Hamman, Robin (1996), *Cyberorgasms: Cybersex amongst Multiple-Selves and Cyborgs in the Narrow Bandwidth Space of America Online Chat Rooms*. MA Dissertation, University of Essex. [WWW doc.] URL http://www.socio.demon.co.uk/Cyborgasms.html [Visit: October 4, 1998]

Hamman, Robin (1998), *The Online/Offline Dichotomy: Debunking Some Myths about AOL Users and the Affects of Their being Online Upon Offline Friendships and Offline Community*. MPhil Dissertation, University of Liverpool. [WWW doc.] URL http://www.cybersoc.com/ [Visit: November 20, 1998]

Hannerz, Ulf (1992), 'The global ecumene as a network of networks', pp. 34-58, in *Conceptualising Society*, Adam Kuper, ed. London, Routledge

Hannerz, Ulf (1996), *Transnational Connections: Culture, people, places*. London, Routledge

Hansen, Klaus Georg (1999), *Mens vi venter: Statusrapport over det første år med verdens nordligste internet café i Innaarsuit*. Arbejdspapir Nr. 141, NORS-Skrifter Nr. 39. Dept. of Geography, Roskilde University

Haraway, Donna. (1985), 'A Manifesto for Cyborgs: Science, Technology, and Socialist Feminism in the 1980s', in *Socialist Review* 15(2): 65-108

Hayden, Linda J. (1999), *How has the Internet Touched You? The Impact of Internet Access on a NWT Community*. MA Thesis, Royal Roads University

Hensel, Chase (1996), *Telling Our Selves: Ethnicity and Discourse in Southwestern Alaska*. Oxford Studies in Anthropological Linguistics: 5. New York, Oxford University Press

ICC (1992) *Principles and Elements for a Comprehensive Arctic Policy*. Montreal: Centre for Northern Studies and Research

Inuit Broadcasting Company (1994), 'Connecting the North Symposium: Defining User's Need', November 23-25, in *The Aboriginal Information Highway*. [WWW doc.] URL http://sae.ca/business/infohiwy/north/foreword.htm [Visit: April 23, 1999]

Jenkins, Richard (1997), *Rethinking Ethnicity: Arguments and Explorations*. London, Sage Publications

Kawagley, Angayuqaq Oscar (1995), *A Yupiaq Worldview*. Prospect Heights, Waveland Press

Kleivan, Helge (1969/70), 'Culture and Ethnic Identity; On Modernisation and Ethnicity in Greenland', in *FOLK* 11-12: 209-231

Lanier, Jaron (1990), 'Riding the Giant Worm to Saturn: Post-Symbolic Communication in Virtual Reality', pp. 186-188 in *Ars Electronica 1990, Vol. 2: Virtuelle Welten*, Gottfried Hattinger et al., eds. Linz, Veritas-Verlag

Lauritsen, Nina (1999), 'Internettet forbinder Grønlands Bygder' *Politiken Erhvervsmagasin,* 3. sektion, 10. februar, side 10

Liep, J & Olwig, K.F (1993), 'Kulturel kompleksitet' in *Komplekse Liv – kulturel mangfoldighed i Danmark*, Liep & Olwig, eds. København, Akademisk Forlag

Lillie, Jonathan James McCreadie (1998), *Cultural Uses of New, Networked Internet Information and Communication Technologies: Implications for US Latino Identities.* Master's Thesis, School of Journalism and Mass Communications, The University of North Carolina. [WWW doc] URL http://metalab.unc.edu/jlillie/thesis.html [Visit: January 19, 1999]

Loader, Brian D. (1997), *The Governance of Cyberspace: Politics, Technology an Global Restructuring*, B. D. Loader, ed. London & New York, Routledge

Lyon, David (1997), 'Cyberspace sociality: Controversies over computer-mediated relationships', pp. 23-37 in *The Governance of Cyberspace*. London, Routledge

Malinowski, Bronislaw (1922), *Argonauts of the Western Pacific: An Account of Native Enterprise and Adventure in the Archipelagos of Melanesian New Guinea*. London, Routledge and Kegan Paul

Malinowski, Bronislaw (1967), *A Diary in the strict sense of the term*. London, Routledge & Kegan Paul

Mitra, Ananda (1997), 'Diasporic Web Sites: Ingroup and Outgroup Discourse', in *Critical Studies in Mass Communication* 14: 158-181

Montaigne, Michel de [1533-1592] (1995), *Four Essays by Michel de Montaigne*, translated by M. A. Screech, Penguin 60th Series. London, Penguin

Negroponte, Nicholas (1995), *Being Digital*. London, Hodder and Stoughton

NEWS/NORTH (1997), 'Wiring the North'. *NEWS/NORTH*, July 28: A22

North, Tim (1994), *The Internet and UseNet Global Computer Networks: An investigation of their culture and its effects on new users*. Master thesis. Perth, Curtin University of Technology. [WWW doc.] URL http://www.vianet.net.au/~timn/thesis/index.html [Visit: December 14, 1998]

Northwestel (1998), *Telecom Public Notice CTRC 97–42, Service to High Cost Serving Areas*, May 1, 1998 Northwestel Inc

Nuttall, Mark (1992), *Arctic Homeland: Kinship, Community and development in Northwest Greenland*. Toronto, Toronto University Press

Olwig, Karen Fog & Kirsten Hastrup (1997), 'Introduction', pp. 1–14 in *Siting Culture: The Shifting Anthropological Object*, Olwig, Karen Fog & Kirsten Hastrup, eds. London, Routledge

Oosten, Jarich & Cornelius Remie, eds. (1999), *Arctic Identities, Continuity and Change in Inuit and Saami Societies*. Research School CNWS, School of Asian, African and Amerindian Studies, Universiteit Leiden

Paccagnella, Luciano (1997), 'Getting the Seats of Your Pants Dirty: Strategies for Ethnographic Research on Virtual Communities', in *Journal of Computer Mediated Communication (JCMC)* 3(1) [WWW doc.] URL http://www.ascusc.org/jcmc/vol3/issue1/paccagnella.html [Vi-sit: December 5, 1998]

Pahl, Raymond Edward (1965), *Urbs in rure. The metropolitan fringe in Hertfordshire*. London School of Economics & Political Science

London Series: London School of Economics and Political Science Geographical Papers. no. 2

Pedersen, Brian Buus (1998), 'Information Technology in Greenland', pp. 225–230 in *POLARTEC '98: International Conference on Development and Commercial Utilisation of Technologies in Polar Regions, Nuuk, Greenland, June 8–14, 1998*

Petersen, Robert (1985), 'The Use of Certain Symbols in Connection with Greenlandic Identity', pp. 294-300 in *Native Power*, Jens Brøsted, et al. Bergen, Universitetsforlaget

Pickard, Meg (1998), *'Under Construction': (re)defining Culture and Community in Cyberspace*. MA Thesis, University of Manchester. [WWW doc.] URL http://members.aol.com/megpic/net/ [Visit: July 28, 1999)

Pitkow, J. E., & Recker, M. M. (1994) 'Using the Web as a survey tool: Results from the second WWW user survey', *Journal of Computer Networks and ISDN Systems*, 27(6)

Postman, Neil (1993), *Technopoly: The Surrender of Culture to Technology*. New York, Vintage Books

Powell, John A. (1997), 'The Multiple Self: Exploring Between and Beyond Modernity and Postmodernity', in *University of Minnesota Law Review 1481*. [WWW doc.] URL http://www1.umn.edu/irp/multiple.htm [Visit: December 4, 1998]

Pullar, Gordon (1992), 'Ethnic Identity, Cultural Pride, and Generations of Baggage: A Personal Experience', in *Arctic Anthropology*, 29(2): 182-191

Qitsualik, Rachel (unknown), No Title. [WWW doc.] URL http://www.cyberus.ca/~stinsley/qletters.htm#tools [Visit: July 27, 1999]

Qitsualik, Rachel (1998), 'Nunani: Cyber-Inuit', in *Nunatsiaq News*, September 24, p.10

Reid, Elizabeth, M. (1991), *Electropolis: Communication and Community on Internet Relay Chat*. Honours Thesis, University of Melbourne

Reid, Elizabeth, M. (1994), *Cultural formations in Text-Based Virtual Reality*. MA Thesis, University of Melbourne. [WWW document] URL http://people.we.mediaone.net/elizrs/cult-form.html [Visit: July 20, 1999]

Reid, Elizabeth, M. (1996), 'Informed Consent in the Study of Online Communities: A Reflection on the Effects of Computer-Mediated Social Research', in *The Information Society*, 12(2). [WWW doc.] URL http://venus.soci.niu.edu/~jthomas/ethics/tis/go.libby [Visit: December 11, 1998]

Rheingold, Howard (1993), *The Virtual Community: Home steading on the Electronic Frontier*. Reading, Mass.: Addison-Wesley Publishing Company

Richardson, Don (1996), *The Internet and Rural Development: Recommendations for Strategy and Activity*. Prepared for the Food and Agriculture Organisation of the United Nations. Guelph, University of Guelph

Richling, Barnett (1989), 'Recent Trends in the Northern Labrador Seal Hunt', in *Etudes/Inuit/Studies*, 9(2): 153-155

Robins, Kevin (1995), 'Cyberspace and the World We Live In', pp. 135-155 in *Cyberspace/Cyberbodies/Cyberpunk: Cultures of Technological Embodiment*, in M. Featherstone & R. Burrows, eds. London, Sage

Sackett, Sydney (1998), 'Iqaluit hockey club to assist Nuuk team', in *Capital News/ Nunatsiaq News*, April 23

Sambo, Dalee (1992), 'Indigenous human rights: The role of Inuit at the United nations Working group on Indigenous Peoples', in *Études/Inuit/Studies*, 16(1-2): 27-32.

Schiller, Herbert I. (1993), *Mass Communication and American Empire*. Boulder, Westview Press

Sejersen, Frank (1994), *Alaska-eskimoer og miljøbevægelse på kollisions-kurs: En analyse af betydninger og opfattelser af hvaler og hvalfangst i Nordalaska*. Speciale [Masters thesis], University of Copenhagen

Sejersen, Frank (1996), 'Arktiske folk som statister og aktører på den globale scene', in *Stofskifte* 32: 41-56

Sejersen, Frank (1998), *Strategies for Sustainability and Management of People: An Analysis of Hunting and Environmental Perceptions in Greenland with a Special Focus on Sisimiut*. PhD dissertation, University of Copenhagen, Denmark

Shucksmith, Mark (1994), 'Conceptualising Post-Industrial Rurality', pp. 125-132 in *Towards Sustainable Rural Communities*, J. M. Bryden, ed.The Guelph Seminar Series

Smith, Christine (1997), 'Casting the Net: Surveying an Internet Population', in *Journal of Computer Mediated Communication (JCMC)*, 3(1). [WWW doc.] URL http://jcmc.huji.ac.il/vol3/issue1/smith.html [Visit: December 3, 1998]

Sprenger, Polly (1999), 'Alaska ISPs Claim Telco Snow Job', in *Wired News*, 27 Feb., 1999

Springer, Claudia (1991), 'The Pleasure of the Interface', in *Screen* 32(3): 303-23

Stenbæk, Marianne (1982), 'Kalaallit-Nunaata Radioa – To be Master of One's Media is to be Master of One's Own Fate', in *Etudes/Inuit/Studies*, 6(1): 39-48

Stenbæk, Marianne (1998a), 'Inuit and Globalisation: Potential Uses of the Internet in the Arctic', pp. 235-240 in *POLARTEC '98: International Conference on Development and Commercial Utilisation of Technologies in Polar Regions*, Nuuk, Greenland, June 8-14, 1998

Stenbæk, Marianne (1998b), 'Sustainable Development and Mass Media in the Arctic: The Case of the Inuit Circumpolar Communications Commission', in H. Petersen & B. Poppel, eds. *Dependency, Autonomy, Sustainability in the Arctic*. Aldershot, Ashgate

Stryde, Rick (1997), 'The ever-expanding Internet', in *NEWS/NORTH*, July 28: A21

Sudweeks, F. & Rafaeli, S. (1995), 'How do you get a hundred strangers to agree? Computer-mediated communication and collaboration,' pp. 115-136 in *Computer networking and scholarship in the 21st century university*, T.M. Harrison & T.D. Stephen, eds. New York, SUNY Press

Talero, Eduardo and Philip Gaudette (1996), *Harnessing Information for Development: A proposal for a Worldbank Group strategy*. Worldbank. [WWW doc.] URL http://www.worldbank.org/html/fpd/harnessing/ [Visit: November 13, 1998]

Teitelbaum, Sheldon (1997), 'The Call of the Wired', in *Wired*, 5(11)

Tele Greenland A/S (1996), *Bestyrelsens beretning ved den ordinære generalforsamling i TELEGreenland A/S*, 15 May 1996

Thomas, Jim (1996), 'When Cyber-Research Goes Awry: The Ethics of the Rimm „Cyberporn" Study', in *The Information Society*, 12(2). [WWW doc.] URL http://venus.soci.niu.edu/~jthomas/ethics/tis/go.jt2 [Vi-sit: December 10, 1998]

Thomas, Lorraine (1998), *Inuktitut and Information Technology*. A discussion paper for the Nunavut Implementation Commission Language Policy Conference

The Information Highway Advisory Council (1995), *Connection, Community, Content. The Challenge of the Information Highway. Final Report of the Information Highway Advisory Council.* Minister of Supply and Services, Canada

Thuesen, Søren (1991), 'Difference and Boundary in a Local Community. On the formation of local associations in West Greenland', *North Atlantic Studies*, 3(1): 46-56

Toennies, F. (1957 [1887]), *Community and Association.* Michigan, Michigan State University Press

Toffler, Alvin (1980), *The Third Wave.* New York, William Morrow

TundraTimes (1996), 'Three Native Corporations join to build 'info-pipeline', in *TundraTimes*, July 17: 5

TundraTimes (1997), 'ASTF wires Schools to Net', in *TundraTimes*, March 12: 1 & 5

Turkle, Sherry (1984), *The Second Self: Computers and the Human Spirit.* New York, Simon and Schuster

Turkle, Sherry (1995), *Life on the Screen: Identity in the Age of the Internet.* New York, Simon and Schuster

UNESCO (1996), *World Science Report.* Paris, UNESCO

Walters, Alison (1996), *An Analysis of Purposes and Forms of Personal Homepages on the World Wide Web.* Thesis, Sloan School of Management Massachusetts Institute of Technology. [WWW doc.] URL http://tranquility.mit.edu/alison/thesis.html [Visit: December 10, 1998]

Waskul, Dennis (1996), 'Ethics of Online Research: Considerations for the Study of Computer Mediated Forms of Interaction', in *The Information Society*, 12(2). [WWW doc.] URL http://venus.soci.niu.edu/~jthomas/ethics/tis/go.dennis. [Visit: December 11, 1998]

Wenzel, George (1986), 'Canadian Inuit in a mixed Economy: Thoughts on seals, snowmobiles and animal rights', in *Native Studies Review*, 2(1): 69-82

Wilkin, Dwane (1998), 'Nortwestel wants $20 to $30 million subsidy', in *Nunatsiaq News,* May 12

Yates & Orlikowski (1992), 'Genres of Organisational Communication: A Structurational Approach to Studying Communication and Media', in *Academy of Management Review*, 17(2): 299–326

Zellen, Barry (1998), 'Surf's up!: NWT's Indigenous Communities Await a Tidal Wave of Electronic Information', in *The Internet and Indigenous Groups. Cultural Survival Quarterly World Report on The Rights of Indigenous Peoples and Ethnic Minorities*. QSQ 21.4. [WWW doc.] URL http://www.ultranet.com/~csinc/csq/csqinternet.html [Visit: November 25, 1998]